Music Education and Muslims

Music Education and Muslims

Diana Harris

Trentham Books

Stoke on Trent, UK and Sterling, USA

Trentham Books Limited

Westview House   22883 Quicksilver Drive
734 London Road   Sterling
Oakhill   VA 20166-2012
Stoke on Trent   USA
Staffordshire
England ST4 5NP

First published 2006

British Library Cataloguing-in-Publication Data
A catalogue record for this book is available from the
British Library

ISBN-10: 1-85856-356-9
ISBN-13: 978-1-85856-356-5

Designed and typeset by Trentham Print Design Ltd., Chester
and printed in Great Britain by Cromwell Press Ltd, Wiltshire.

Contents

1
Introduction

When I began my research into the issues surrounding the teaching of music to Muslims, I felt like the hobbit Bilbo Baggins sitting on the doorstep of the door to The Lonely Mountain. 'No sign was there of post or lintel or threshold, nor any sign of bar or bolt or keyhole; yet they did not doubt that they had found the door at last' (Tolkien, 1937 p190). I was not even sure I had found the right door and at times even questioned whether there was one. As my research progressed I discovered that there were actually several doors or gates, all of them open a tantalising crack, and many of the gatekeepers were offering me a cautious welcome. Since then I have often felt humbled by the remarkable warmth and trust extended to me by Muslims in both England and abroad. It is because of the welcome I have received from them that I feel justified in presenting my research in this book.

The story began in 1991 when I took up a post as Head of Performing Arts at a girls' high school in Luton, where most of the pupils were Muslim. Whilst it cannot be assumed that all Muslims have an issue with performing arts, music, dance and drama in schools, there has been sufficient unease in Muslim communities for it to merit attention. Music presents an ethical dilemma for some Muslims and this needs to be recognised. It manifests itself most obviously at secondary school level and is observable in various ways. On a day to day basis, at Key Stage 3, there were girls who only mimed in class singing lessons, constantly forgot their kit for dance lessons and hid behind their shyness in drama. But the problems became increasingly obvious when pupils opted for performing arts at Key Stage 4 or wanted to take part in extra curricular activities. What do you say to parents at a Parents' Evening about their daughter who is taking dance as a key component in GCSE Expressive Arts and has pleaded with you: 'Don't tell my parents I dance'? What can you say to a talented flute player who can no longer play now she is a 'woman'? And how can you maintain the tradition of large scale school productions when the keen participants return the consent forms unsigned because their parents refuse to give permission?

What I am *not* trying to do, never have nor ever will do, is to try to persuade anyone to do something they feel is wrong. However, the more I consider this subject the more I realise that within Islam there is a huge and diverse range of opinions. The people I have talked to and the books I have read have convinced me that there is no one right answer where music is concerned. But I hope that in helping Muslims to become more aware of the favourable opinions about music, I am offering them the opportunity to reconsider their attitudes and, if they come to see music as acceptable, enable them and their children to share in what is for me one of the most amazing things the world has to offer.

Why is music important? And, why teach music? Apart from it being wonderful what else has it to offer? Talking with my supervisor I insisted that my doctoral thesis was about performing arts rather than just music. What is important is not music or dance or drama *per se*: trying to get Muslims to understand or appreciate a Brahms symphony is not the point. What I am interested in is helping them experience the liberating power, the creative potential and the capacity for self-expression which come with the ability to respond to, or take part in, performing arts. I am interested in the concepts of self esteem and individual autonomy. My supervisor replied that if I saw music or performing arts as a trigger to an experience then there may be other triggers that could do the same thing. Music may not be the only way to engage with these ideas, and maybe there is something universally accepted in Islam that could do so. But it is music that I understand and, more mundanely, it is music which is a compulsory part of the National Curriculum in the UK until the age of 14. In my enthusiasm to pursue my objective of opening up music to more pupils, I sometimes have to keep myself in check and remember Bowman's comment (2005), 'Is what we desire, desirable?' He continued, 'To separate music research from the social and the political is appalling'. For this reason it seems important to know as much as possible about Islam itself, and how it is lived in the modern world.

A brief look at the Islamic concept of education from a historical perspective reveals why music does not fit readily into its curriculum. Most education in medieval times was seen largely as the provenance of religious organisations. In the 9th century the *madrasa*, the place of study, became the centre of learning for Muslims. The *madrasas* only taught the Qur'an, *ahadith* (the reported sayings of the Prophet), *fiqh* (jurisprudence) and Arabic language; no other forms of knowledge were considered legitimate and so were unacceptable. The object of education was to prepare people so they could acquire *sa'ada* (bliss) in the after-life. Although other subjects have now entered the curriculum, as Talbani (1996 p69), wrote:

> Knowledge above that minimally required to meet daily social and economic needs [is] considered dangerous.

Halstead (2004, p518), agreed:

> ...popular Muslim opinion has tended to the view that anything outside the divine truth of the Qur'an is at best superficial (there being enough in the Qur'an to constitute a perfectly balanced education), and at worst dangerous, since the study of philosophy and other non-Islamic sciences could lead believers astray from the true path.

However, the Association of Muslim Social Scientists (2004, p11) wrote:

> In Islam, the purpose of education is to impart beneficial forms of knowledge in a manner that will help the individual attain success in this life and the next. In more contemporary terminology, such an observation might suggest that in Islam there is a requirement for both temporal and spiritual knowledge.

It went on to quote from the Recommendation of the First World Conference on Muslim Education (1977), which stated: 'Education should aim at the balanced growth of the total personality of man though the training of man's spirit, intellect, the rational self, feelings and bodily senses'. It is important to understand the Islamic meaning of 'knowledge' and 'education'. Knowledge (*ta'lim*) is confined to two categories: it is either to be found directly in the Qur'an, or it is directly related to a specific purpose in life. In an Islamic context knowledge has to have a reason; it cannot be acquired for its own sake. However, the Qur'an states that the pursuit of knowledge is an obligation for all men and women, and that it must be continued throughout life, always remembering that it applies only to knowledge which will lead to *sa'ada*.

3

Knowledge itself comes in two forms: revealed (*naqliyyah*) and humanly constructed (*'aqliyya*) but in both forms revolves around the Qur'an. Gaining knowledge, of whatever type, must lead to a better understanding of the Qur'an, and this can only come from learned scholars. Also,

> Islam encourages an attitude of respectful humility towards legiti-
> mate authority and trust in the truth of knowledge that it hands
> down... there is no justification for encouraging children to question
> their faith. (Halstead, 2004, p525)

Thirdly, knowledge is not separate from other aspects of society; it is firmly fixed in the *umma* (community) and directly related to pre-serving values and beliefs.

Education itself is divided into three types: acquisition of knowledge (*ta'lim*), individual development (*tarbiya*), from the Arabic root *raba* meaning to grow or increase, and character development (*ta'dib*), from the root *aduba* meaning to be refined or cultured. *Tarbiya* is concerned with developing the potential of each individual, and *ta'dib* is directly related to developing moral character within the *umma* or community. All these forms of education can be found in the *shari'a*, the law based on the Qur'an, and are not open to individual interpretation. Therefore, as Halstead points out:

> In Islam... there is no question of individuals being encouraged
> through education to work out for themselves their own religious
> faith or to subject it to detached rational investigation at a funda-
> mental level; the divine revelation expressed in the *shari'a* provides
> them with the requisite knowledge of truth and falsehood, right and
> wrong, and the task of individuals is to come to understand this
> knowledge and exercise their free will to choose the path to follow.
> (*ibid*, p523)

These meanings of education and knowledge differ significantly from the western concept, which has moved away from the idea of education as communicating facts to a passive audience, to a belief that questioning is healthy and that all forms of learning have a place. And since 'certainty curtails enquiry' (Bowman, 2005), there is less enquiry in the Islamic curriculum than in a Western one. As Abdullah wrote (quoted in Talbani, 1996, p76) of Islamic education:

> The superiority of revealed knowledge is due to the fact that it is
> derived from the truth (*haqq*), while some other types of knowledge
> are based on speculation (*zann*), or desires (*hawa*).

If Islamic education needs to be based on a particular truth imparted by learned scholars and cannot include either speculation or the desire to find out for yourself, where does it leave the question of music education?

Needing real dialogue about the place of music in the education of Muslims is symptomatic of the need for a broader dialogue about the place of Muslims in Western society. Islamophobia is a serious barrier to this. Islamophobia is not new: the European Monitoring Centre on Racism and Xenophobia report of 2002 suggested that the bombings of 9/11 had the effect of reaffirming old prejudices about Islam, as well as fuelling new fears amongst non-Muslims. The anger and frustration of many young Muslims is clear. As Stone (2004, pvii) put it:

> Today, Britain's 1.6 million Muslims are living on a diet of death, hypocrisy and neglect that is traumatising and radicalising an entire generation.

It is not just the younger generation who are being traumatised. Many Muslims are trying to hide their 'Muslimness' because of fear of reprisals from non-Muslims. As a temporary solution Zaki Badawi 'issued a *fatwa* that Muslim women in Britain have an Islamic right to take off their *hijab* at this point of time if attacked or fearing to be attacked' (reported by IslamOnline.net). An anonymous Muslim advocated that 'carrying a bottle of wine on the underground would mean they were not suspected of terrorism'. These suggestions have understandably been descried by many Muslims but it is fair to say that Western society has traumatised Muslims. This leads to the trap I have just fallen into by making the generalisation that Western society is anti-Islam. But Allen (2004), wrote:

> The distinctions between religion and ethnicity, therefore, became increasingly blurred, and the primacy of an enemy's Muslimness, whether relevant or not, was stressed in order to reinvigorate and reaffirm historical foes, albeit in a contemporary frame of reference and understanding. (p6)

Muslims should never be treated as an undifferentiated mass. One outstandingly individual and powerful speaker is Tariq Ramadan. Ramadan, cited by *Time Magazine* as one of the world's 100 most influential thinkers, is certain that the only way forward for Muslims living in the West is to 'reach out and create partnerships' (Bunting, 2004). Although Ramadan has given a presentation to the US State Department about European Muslims, in July 2004 he was refused a visa to take up a professorship in the Peace Studies Department of the Notre Dame University in Indiana as he was thought to support Islamic extremism. Many Muslims also have contradictory views about him. Although some critics accuse him of betraying Islam he stands firm in his belief that:

> A silent revolution is coming in how Muslims think about themselves and about the universal common values they share with the West, and about democracy and modernity...the development of a European Islam will have a tremendous impact on Islam throughout the world. (Ramadan, 2004)

In Chapter 2 Ramadan's views about music are discussed in the wider context of whether Islam and the West can live side by side. The Muslim Public Affairs Council (2005) reported his comments that Muslim communities in the West need to take steps to 'face down literal interpretations of the Qur'an that bear no relationship to modern life', and that 'young Muslims must break out of an Eastward-looking social and intellectual ghetto and go it alone'. This suggests that Muslims might be encouraged to ask questions and think for themselves, and perhaps eventually come to Barenboim's view that 'Music is not about statements or about being. It's about becoming' (2002, p21).

Can this best be done from within the state education sector, whether faith schools or not, or from within Islamic independent schools? Following the Labour Government's decision to encourage faith schools in the UK (Home Office Faith Communities Unit, 2004), more British Muslim schools have been requesting Voluntary Aided status. Walford (2003) compared England with the Netherlands, noting that in the Netherlands 34 were state funded, as against only four out of the over 60 Muslim schools in England. Many Muslims believe that faith schools are the only sensible way forward. In a letter to the Secretary of State for Education (2005), Ahmad, from the London School of Islamics, wrote:

> Muslim children in state schools feel isolated and confused about who they are. This can cause dissatisfaction and lead them into criminality, and the lack of a true understanding of Islam can ultimately make them more susceptible to the teachings of fundamentalists, like Christians during the middle ages and Jews in recent times in Palestine. Fundamentalism is nothing to do with Islam and Muslim; you are either a Muslim or a non-Muslim... 97% of Muslim pupils are in state schools. There are hundreds of state schools where Muslim pupils are in the majority. In my opinion all such schools may be converted to Muslim community schools,

managed and controlled by Muslim Educational Trusts or Charities. State funded Muslim schools make sense. This means the Muslim children will get a decent education. Muslim schools turn out balanced citizens, more tolerant of others and less likely to succumb to criminality or extremism.

Faith schools funded by the state would, however, still be subject to government requirements. As Walford wrote in an earlier report:

> State funding brings disadvantages as well as advantages...funding has been associated with considerable state control and regulation over aspects such as curriculum, staffing, admissions criteria, inspection and governance. (2001, p359)

So although Muslim schools are being encouraged to seek state funding, many prefer to remain independent so they can control what is taught. In one unfortunate school the argument between those in favour of state funding and those against meant that the school ended up being closed altogether.

This book began with the intention of helping teachers in state schools to provide a music curriculum more acceptable for their Muslims pupils. After many conversations with teachers from independent Muslim schools I am hoping that music will soon be on the curriculum in more of them as well. But it may be some time before we can promote Barenboim's (2002 p21) idea that, '...one of the reasons why artistic creation is so important today is that it is a total opposite of being politically correct, of being uncontroversial'.

Chapter 2 offers an historical view of music and Islam and outlines why music has become problematic for some Muslims. Chapter 3 is based on my conversations with Muslim religious leaders, teachers, scholars and musicians over the past six years about their attitudes towards Islam, and what music means to them. It begins with some general points about Islam but deals mostly with views on the controversial aspects of music. Importantly it reveals the wide range of opinions amongst Muslims.

Chapter 4, which a friend calls: 'What I have done on my holidays', looks at the countries where I did my fieldwork – Pakistan, Egypt and Turkey – and gives relevant information about their education system, with interviews and observations derived during my fieldwork. There is also information from Malaysia, Finland, USA and Canada, contributed by my contacts in those countries. The chapter shows clearly the diversity of opinion on music and Islam within the *umma* and considers experiences of music education to people from Islamic countries who have moved to the West. Chapter 5 is devoted to an in-depth case study of a family living in Pakistan and UK.

Chapters 6 and 7 are concerned with music in schools in the UK. Chapter 6 is a case study of a school in a Midlands city in which I was a participant observer. It provides insight into what was done about music education in a state funded secondary school with a majority of Muslim pupils. Chapter 7 looks at two on-going studies. The first has been set up to help Muslim teachers who want to teach music in their Islamic school; the second has a wider brief to bring music from Islamic cultures into state school music lessons. The final chapter, Chapter 8, is designed to address the question of how to help both Muslim and non-Muslim teachers who want to encourage music suitable for Muslims in school. The chapter concludes with a list of resources that I have found useful and relevant.

2

Music and Islam

slam was begun by the Prophet Muhammad in the 7th century. When he died his followers split into two groups, the Shias or Shi'ites, and the Sunnis. The Shias believed that the leader of their new faith should be a direct descendant of the Prophet, whereas the Sunnis believed that leadership should be based on spirituality. This split continues to this day. Within these two major groups are many denominations among whom are the Sufis. In this book I tend to discuss Islam as a whole, the similarities in the sects being far greater than the differences. But within the field of music the Sufis take a particular position.

All Islamic thought and action is based on three sources. The first is the Qur'an, revealed by Allah to the Prophet Muhammad. The second is the body of literature forming the *ahadith (hadith* in the singular), the reported sayings of the Prophet handed down by word of mouth, and mostly recorded during the two centuries after his death. These can be divided into those which are generally acknowledged to be sound and those which are not. They are analogous to the Christian Gospels that recount the story of Jesus but were also not written down during his lifetime. The third source is the *sunnah:* the reported actions of the Prophet also found in the *ahadith*. The sayings and actions of the Prophet gave an example to his followers, but just because the Prophet did not do something himself it does not mean that it is necessarily *haram* (forbidden). For example, it is sufficient for the Prophet to have seen something and not commented negatively on it for it to be considered *mubah* (acceptable).

It is generally agreed that there is no mention of music in the *Qur'an*. However, some scholars have, controversially, interpreted the Qur'an reference to 'idle talk' as a condemnation of music:

> There are among men those who purchase idle talk in order to mislead others from Allah's path without knowledge, and who throw ridicule upon it. (Surah Luqmaan: 06)

According to some academics and religious leaders, 'idle talk' in this instance means either singing and listening to songs, or purchasing of male and female singers, or purchasing musical instruments of pleasure.

Raza (1991, p60) wrote 'the community misinterprets Islam according to their needs', and there are many passages in the *hadith* which descry music. Those often quoted include: 'Singing sprouts hypocrisy in the heart as rain sprouts plants' (al Baihaqi, in Lambat, 1998); 'Musical instruments are amongst the most powerful means by which the devil seduces human beings' (Farmer, 1973); and 'The person who sings, and the person who listens to singing, both are cursed by Allah' (Sha'bi, quoted in Hassan, 1993). These, however, are not generally considered to be 'sound' hadith, meaning that the line from the Prophet to the hadith writer has at some time been broken, or that the writer lacks sufficient authority to make the claim. Maqsood (interview 17th June 1999) explained *ahadith* as follows:

> There are thousands and thousands of *hadith* which are very very weak, if not meaningless. They have to be in keeping with the spirit of the Qur'an. Now nowhere in the Qur'an does it forbid music. So therefore I suspect some of them straight away. When you are my kind of Muslim you always go back to the Qur'an. If God wanted to forbid a certain thing he would have said so but there's no mention in the Qur'an of forbidding music. When you look at the *hadith* you have to look at who said them and why they said them. I can't think of a single *hadith* condemning music which is a strong one they are all weak. And it's a well known fact, although Muslims don't like to admit it, that many *hadiths* were just invented for pious reasons.

Two *ahadith* from reliable sources are less easy to explain in terms of their apparent opposition to music. Ibn Majah (in al Qaradawi, 1960, p304) reported the Prophet as saying:

> Some of my *umma* (Muslim community), will drink wine, calling it by another name, while they listen to singers accompanied by musical instruments. Allah will cause the earth to swallow them and will turn some of them into monkeys and swine.

and al Bukhari (n.d) quoted the Prophet as saying:

> There will be people from my *umma* who will seek to make lawful fornication, the wearing of silk by men, wine drinking and the use of musical instruments.

About both of these examples more moderate scholars (eg. al Qaradawi, see below) argue that it is not the musical instruments which are the problem but the association with things which *are* forbidden, namely alcohol and fornication. And Ibn Hazm (*ibid* p302) quotes al Bukhari to show that he was not totally averse to music in an appropriate setting:

> The Messenger of Allah (peace be on him) said, 'Deeds will be judged according to intentions, and everyone will get what he intended.' Accordingly, the one who listens to singing with the intention of using it in support of a sin is a sinner, and this holds true of anything other than singing (as well), while one who listens to singing with the intention of refreshing his soul in order to gain strength to do his duty toward Allah *Ta'ala* and to do good deeds, is a good and obedient servant of Allah, and his action is the truth. And he who listens to singing intending neither obedience nor disobedience is doing something neutral and harmless, which is similar to going to the park and walking around, standing by a window and looking at the sky, wearing blue or green clothes, and so on'.

al Qaradawi (1960 p 300) quoted the following as being reported by al Bukhari and Ibn Majah:

> Aishah [the Prophet's wife] narrated that when a woman was married to an Ansari man, the Prophet (peace be upon him) said, 'Aishah, did they have any entertainment? The Ansari are fond of entertainment.' 'No', said Aishah. The Messenger of Allah (peace be upon him) then said, 'The Ansar are a people who love poetry. You should have sent someone along who would sing'.

There are many reported instances of the Prophet listening to music and this action is held by moderate scholars to confirm music as being acceptable in some circumstances. For example, al Qaradawi (*op cit*, p300), quoting al Bukhari and Muslim, wrote:

> Aishah narrated that during the days of Mina, on the day of '*Eid al-Adha*, two girls were with her, singing and playing on a hand drum. The Prophet (peace be upon him) was present, listening to them with his head under a shawl. Abu Bakr then entered and scolded the girls. The Prophet (peace be upon him), uncovering his face, told him, 'Let them be, Abu Bakr. These are the days of 'Eid'.

The debate about whether music is permissible or not continues. al Qaradawi (1960 p290) wrote:

> Islam does not require of Muslims that their speech should consist entirely of pious utterances, that their silence should be a meditation, that they should listen to nothing except the recitation of the Qur'an, nor that they should spend all their leisure time in the mosque.

He believes that singing is permissible under certain conditions. He makes five points (*ibid* p303):

- The subject matter of songs should not be against the teachings of Islam. For example, if the song is in praise of wine and it invites people to drink, singing or listening to it is *haram*.

- Although the subject matter itself may not be against the Islamic teachings, the manner of singing may render it *haram*; this would be the case, for example, if the singing were accompanied by suggestive sexual movement.

- Islam fights against excess and extravagance in anything, even in worship; how, then, can it tolerate excessive involvement with entertainment?

- Each individual is the best judge of himself. If a certain type of singing arouses one's passions, leads him towards sin, excites the animal instincts, and dulls spirituality, he must avoid it, thus closing the door to temptations.

- There is unanimous agreement that if singing is done in conjunction with *haram* activities it is *haram*.

How, then, according to classic interpretations contained in the four main legal schools in Sunni Islam, has it been agreed that the testimony of a singer is not admissible as evidence in court? In the Shafie law manual it is mentioned that the testimony of singers (along with scavengers, rag gathers, sweepers, bath-men, dancers and jugglers) may not be used and is to be rejected. However, Shirazi, Ruzbahan Baqli (nd) *On the Meaning of Spiritual Music* (in Tahir, 1998) believes that all creatures have a natural inclination towards spiritual music as each of us has a spirit. Spiritual music may be said to be of three kinds: one for the common people (who listen through nature), another for the elite (who listen with the heart) and a third for the elite among elite (who listen with the soul). For people to be able to listen to music someone must perform it. But since musical instruments are more controversial, it is perhaps understandable that a legal reference in al Qayrawani (Russell, 1906 p92) says that the hand of a thief should not be cut off for stealing musical instruments because they are 'sinful tools', and that the breaking of musical instruments is lawful and should incur no penalty.

Isma'il and Lois Ibsen al Faruqi lived and worked in America during the1980s. Lois dealt specifically with music whilst her husband wrote about culture and the arts in general. There has been speculation that their research and writing may have been a reason why they were both murdered but no evidence has been found to corroborate this. Of particular relevance to this chapter are their publications *Music, Musicians and Muslim Law* and *The Shar'ia on Music and Musicians*. Lois al Faruqi believed that it was important to avoid the term 'music' because, if used at all in Muslim countries, it generally denotes non-religious music. The term she preferred was *handasah al sawt*, literally 'sound arts'. All actions in Islam fall into five categories: compulsory, recommended, allowed/tolerated, disapproved and forbidden; al Faruqi produced a table showing the hierarchy of *handasah al sawt* genres as she saw them. She began with Qur'anic Chant, which is the only form that is truly *halal*, or compulsory. There follow the areas that are recommended: religious chants, the chants of pilgrims and chants of praise and thanks. In the allowed/tolerated section are family celebrations, work songs and military music (although some people would also put the music that accompanies soldiers going to war into the compulsory or recommended sections). Improvisatory music, serious metred songs, instrumental music and music related to pre or non-Islamic origins would generally be disapproved of. All sensuous music and all music heard or performed in unacceptable contexts would be forbidden.

Although in practice many Muslims perceive there to be a distinction between listening and performing, al Faruqi (*ibid*, p16), said that no distinction is made in Islamic law. She wrote:

> It should be noted that the performer of *musiqa* (non religious music) has generally been accorded no better or no worse treatment than the listener. Both socially and legally, there has been little differentiation between the attitude toward musicians, on the one hand, and listeners or patrons on the other.

What are very important, however, are the *zaman* (time), *makan* (place) and *ikhwan* (associates) of the *handasah al sawt* activity. She continued (*ibid*, p17):

> al Ghazali reasoned that life is a serious matter that allows little time for frivolous entertainment. Therefore, he argued that if a musician

(or listener) devoted too much time to *sawti* (entertainment), such activities became a detriment rather than an innocent pastime.

For this reason professional musicians have often been treated with disdain, whereas non-professionals have been tolerated. And ironically, a professional musician will gain respect only if performing religious music, but cannot be paid: it is unacceptable to be paid for something which it is a religious duty to perform.

The current debate

A conference was run by The Association of Muslim Researchers in 1993 entitled *Much Ado About Music* (Proceedings, 1996) at the Royal College of Music, to discuss the implications of music being made a compulsory subject in the National Curriculum for children up to the age of 14. The views of the five speakers invited to contribute papers ranged across the whole spectrum of Islamic opinion on music. Two of these speakers are established authorities on Islam: Zaki Badawi, principal of the Muslim College in London and previously director of the Regents Park Mosque; and Suhaib Hasan, lecturer and writer on the teachings of the Qu'ran and *hadiths*. The others are more recent converts to Islam: Ibrahim Hewitt has worked for the Muslim Educational Trust and was Developmental Officer for the Association of Muslim Schools for several years; Abd al-Rahman Johansen, a graduate in Arabic and a lawyer who has written extensively on Sufism in particular, and Abd al-Lateef Whiteman, an architect who is also a musician and has branched out into producing documentaries, designing books and singing *qasidahs* (sung poetry).

What all participants agreed was that music as such could not be declared illegal. In her introduction (AMR, 1996, p12), Haulkhory wrote: 'Declaring a prohibition on music would be tantamount to prohibiting nature from manifesting itself'. The question of allowing musical instruments was problematic. Hasan argued that there was no room for compromise on musical instruments and that all were *haram*. Hewitt agreed with this argument but in his paper *Orchestrating Laxity*, he justified his rejection of musical instruments because they might lead by association to *haram* activities, which are illegal.

> ...any activity which engenders, is suggestive of, or encourages behaviour or talk that is contrary to Islamic teachings is considered to be forbidden. (*ibid,* p48)

None of the participants disagreed with this. But Hewitt goes further by suggesting that people are incapable of making up their own minds.

> Music also must have its limit, and that limit has been clearly defined by the Prophet. It nips the problem in the bud – musical instruments must be avoided. (*ibid,* p54)

Badawi, Johansen and Whiteman were all more accepting of musical instruments within certain guidelines. Badawi based his paper on aspects of contention in the jurisprudence about the nature of music. Discussing the various schools of thought, he made the point that:

> ...the only person whose words cannot ever be challenged is the Prophet Muhammad. Anyone else should be treated with respect, but not as though all their words are beyond doubt. (*ibid,* p25)

Another major strand in his argument concerned the Muslim fear of *bid'ah* (innovation). According to Islam, innovation in matters of the Qu'ran is *haram*, but this has been interpreted by some scholars to mean that any innovation is wrong. Badawi wrote:

> Many of the present arguments against music are symptomatic of a broader underlying attitude – that of a blind rejection of the new; a refusal of modernity in its every aspect. (*ibid,* p19)

Badawi concluded that it is up to individuals to look to their own consciences and agree to differ on matters that are not crucial or basic to Islam. He took musical instruments to be a case in point. Johansen and Whiteman concurred with this view.

Following on from the 1993 conference, a conference in London in 2002 looked specifically at the situation regarding music and Muslims in schools. Key to this event was the paper of Tariq Ramadan. Born in Switzerland of Egyptian heritage, Ramadan is a philosopher who has spent his life trying to reconcile Islam with living in the West. His views about music are clearly thought out:

> From my reading and studying Muslim views about music and Islam I have come to the opinion that there will never be a definite and common answer to this question, and what we have to deal with is the diversity within Muslim cultures.

He explained that although Islam is a universal message it must be looked at within the context of the different cultures where Muslims live. This means that there is a need to extract the Islamic principles from the cultural reading of them; dealing with music is much, much more complex than just a matter of jurisprudence. But there is no one correct interpretation of Islamic texts. Different *ulama* have read the same Qur'anic verses in different ways. Ramadan stated that 'In my view it is important to respect all the different views, providing they fall within the framework of Islam'.

Ramadan differs from many Islamic scholars in his belief that Muslims need to adapt to the culture of the Western country that they have chosen to live in.

> Within Islam there is an ethics of culture and an ethics of citizenship. In moving to a different country a person comes with their principles, and should stick to their principles, but they also have to take account of principles in the field of social participation, political participation and cultural participation in the new country.

His final point was that music is a question of conscience and that it should be personal and individual. Music education is particularly important in order to help Muslim pupils build up a 'critical, selective and creative mind'.

This chapter indicates some of the ambiguity and controversy surrounding the issue of music in Islam, and the debate has been limited to a small number of academics and religious leaders. In the next chapter I take this discussion forward in conversations I had with Muslims from various backgrounds.

3
Conversations with Muslims

This chapter contains extracts from the many interesting Muslims I interviewed who contributed to my understanding of attitudes towards music and the variety of opinion that exists towards aspects of Islam in general. For this reason I divided it into two sections. The first deals with general points about Islam and looks at its adaptability and universality. The bulk of the chapter considers aspects more specifically about music: the range of cultural and religious views; reasons for and against music; issues about performing and professional musicians; spiritual and emotional issues; and creativity. Conversations about making the curriculum more inclusive in order to encourage more Muslim participation are incorporated into Chapter 8.

The interviewees are listed in chronological order, the interviews having happened between 1999 and 2005. Comments from interviewees who have seen the final version of the chapter have sometimes been incorporated but it was not possible to give everyone the 'right to reply'.

Ruqaiyyah Waris Maqsood (Sister Ruqaiyyah)

Sr Ruqaiyyah was an RE teacher in Hull for many years. She has now retired from the classroom and has become well-known as a writer on Islamic issues. She has over 40 published books, mainly for young people and new converts. She still tutors privately in the Islamic options of Religious Studies GCSE.

Mohammad Iqbal (pseudonym)

Iqbal is the headmaster of a Muslim independent school who does not want to have his comments attributed.

Asaf Hussain

Hussain is a Pakistani academic who teaches courses of Islamic civilization at the University of Leicester. His area of interest is Islamic fundamentalism and terrorism and he has met many such groups in the Middle East and South Asia. He is currently writing a book on Islamic Fundamentalism in Britain.

Siraj (ibn) Yusuf Lambat (pseudonym)

Lambat is the author of *Music Exposed*, a book denouncing music of every kind, whom I interviewed at the home of an imam.

Ibrahim Hewitt

Hewitt became a Muslim in his early twenties. At the time of interviewing him he ran the Association of Muslim Schools, whose role is to co-ordinate both the independent Muslim schools and the Muslim state schools. Before becoming a Muslim he was actively involved with music.

Imam Shahid Raza

Imam Raza graduated in biology and chemistry from a university in India, then took a postgraduate degree in Islamic studies. After working in Leicester he went to the Muslim College in London, in charge of training imams, but continues to lead the prayers at Leicester Central Mosque on Fridays. He is now the executive secretary of the Muslim Law Council, based at the Muslim College, handling up to fifty phone calls a day on questions of Islamic theology and Muslim ways of life. He has also been an imam at the Central Mosque in Regent's Park, London.

Abd al-Lateef Whiteman

Whiteman became a Muslim when he was twenty-five. He trained as an architect but was always very involved with music. He now works from home designing 'anything you can on a computer': books, corporate identities, advertising, even buildings. He is still a practising musician and in 1997 sang in a concert with Yusuf Islam, formerly Cat Stevens, in Bosnia.

Abd'Allah Trevathan

Trevathan, an American convert to Islam, is the head teacher at Islamia Primary School in London. Islamia is a Muslim state school in England and as such is required to follow the National Curriculum. Yusuf Islam started Islamia.

Sheikh Ahmed

Ahmed was born in Sudan and studied Islam from the age of seven whilst also attending normal school. After school he studied management and mathematics in England because as well as being a Sheikh he needed to be able to earn a living. He expected to go back to Sudan but was encouraged to stay and work in England. He became a teacher and now teaches at Islamia as well as being their resident imam.

Michéle Massaoudi

Massaoudi is French but has been working in England for thirty-four years. Since becoming a Muslim she has worked only with Muslim organisations, following a pledge she made when she turned to Islam. She has mainly worked in education but also in publishing, and at the time I interviewed her had a temporary contract as Head of the Avenue School in London. Avenue is a Muslim independent school but since she was keen to develop music, she devised a music curriculum for Muslim primary schools.

Najma Ahktar

Akhtar is a Muslim born and brought up in England, her parents' country of origin being India. She has a degree and masters qualifications in chemical engineering but now works as a vocalist, songwriter and lecturer at the Westminster University, where she is the module leader for a world music course. She has performed with her band all over the world and has recorded a number of albums. Akhtar is known for creating a new world music sound of traditional Indian music with jazz.

Reem Kelani

Kelani is a Palestinian who was born in Manchester and brought up in Kuwait. She returned to the UK in 1989. She is a successful solo singer who also runs workshops about Arabic and Palestinian music. Kelani has recorded old women in refugee camps in the diaspora and in her native Nazareth and surrounding region of Galilee.

Mustapha Styer

Styer is an American who has been teaching music at the Suffah Primary School in Hounslow. He is interested in setting up a website so that more Muslims interested in teaching music can find resources readily.

Islam

> Islam is a universal religion; its universality comes from the fact that it is adaptable to every day and age, not because it should be the same in every day and age. The universality of Islam is its adaptability, not its rigidity. (Reem Kelani)

Kelani's view of Islam is my reason for being positive about a religion which many people in the Western world see as negative. But because it is adaptable a plethora of different practices exist. Raza, the most senior of the imams I interviewed, put it this way:

> Islam is ... a world wide way of life and what I have understood after studying Islam for such a long time now is that Islam has never been against local customs and traditions in totality. The approach of Islam has always been to accept these fundamental basic principles of Islam and then stay in your own cultural environment. Islam has never been seen as a very rigid or narrow sort of religion which demands that once you are a Muslim you have to leave everything, you have to undergo a complete transformation in every respect.

Looking at the relationship between Islam and music is problematic because there are many different interpretations of the Qur'an and the *ahadith*. Sr Ruqaiyyah:

> There are many schools of thought in Islam and most people are only aware of one. They do not know about the points of view of the other ones, just like in Christianity you've got the Salvation Army banging their tambourines and Quakers and Roman Catholics.

The two branches of Islam are the Shia and the Sunni. Ahmed said that the Shia and Sunni agree on everything: 'The creator, the messenger, the link to all other messengers, the link to other books, the Qur'an, everything', but in practice the differences often seem more apparent than the similarities. In the two centuries following the birth of Islam the Muslims went to live in many different parts of the world and established their own set of rules. Hussian believes that one problem over-rides issues of Shia and Sunni:

You have got to know the schisms that are going on. One Muslim might say, 'This music is allowed, this is not', but you have to remember that at this point that I am talking to you the whole Muslim world is in a state of turmoil. Everything is being debated.

Christians are ruled by their clergy but in Islam there are no clergy as such, only leaders. Imams run the Mosques and Sheikhs give the sermons and take the prayers on Fridays. According to Massaoudi, this means that there are many different points of view. She said:

The reason for this is that within a very broad avenue, and it's not for nothing that the Arabic word to mean law, sharia, also means avenue, within an avenue you can be at any point on the breadth of that avenue and you are still within Islam. So Islam can accommodate a variety of opinions, all of them with validity, depending on the context and the area where they are expressed.

The largest group of Muslims in England are the Sunnis. The Sufis are usually seen as a branch of the Sunnis but, according to Raza, the Sufis do not always agree with this:

...the Sufis do not claim that they are a separate tradition against Sunnis, they claim that they are the real Sunnis, they are the only Sunnis and the others, who are not Sufis, they term the Mujwaharis. The Waharis originated in Saudi Arabia, that's how the Sufis see the different movements within the history of Islam.

As well as theological differences there are also cultural differences between Muslims. Sr Ruqaiyyah pointed out,

...most people tend to think of Muslims as just being either Asians or Arabs, they don't realise that you can be an Eskimo to be a Muslim, or Chinese, or from Finland, or Bosnia – really wherever you go there are Muslims. It's a faith not a culture but the culture is soaked into it. It's the same Islam but the cultures are so different.

In my research, I found that a key question amongst the people I interviewed was: Should Muslims who move to the West adopt Western ways or keep to the traditions in the Islamic state they came from? Hewitt does not believe it is Muslims who should change even though he was born here.

There is the route we could go down which says we must change because this is not a Muslim country. Or, we say, this is a non-Muslim country so we have the opportunity to give them Islam. To show them what the benefits of Islam are. Does that mean we have to change ourselves or does that mean we have to try to change what we have surrounding us? I would say that we have to change what is around us.

Because I am interested primarily in music teaching in the UK, Massaoudi feels that I should restrict my interviewees to those who know about education. She thinks I may 'come across sections of the Muslim population that live as they would live in other parts of the world and are not really addressing issues related to education in the UK'. Cultural problems are often exacerbated by immigrants bringing imams over from their home communities. They feel the need to do this because they often cannot understand the language of the imams already here. Sr Ruqaiyyah says that what is required are well trained imams with degrees who understand English and psychology and are, 'all the things you'd expect from a super-duper vicar'. Raza agrees:

> Many Muslims are living, say, in a street in Bradford physically but mentally they are still living on a road in Mirpur or in Gujarat in India. And that has caused so many problems for the families of the Muslim community. An imam who cannot speak English, who has no first hand knowledge of the British society, will not be, unfortunately and sadly, able to play his role properly.

Hussain said that it is important to remember that some Muslims are looking forward and others back. *Taqlid*, meaning imitation, are the Muslims who are looking to the past, whilst others allow independent reasoning. He believes that it is impossible to go back to the Prophet's time and people must look forward, but this is a threat to many local imams; they want to keep everything in their local community exactly as it was. Hussain believes this must change because looking backwards is not working:

> It is a great threat to the local imam who is a man who comes from the *madrassa*, and is educated on a very simplistic level. There are problems in the Muslim community and the newspapers can bear witness. There are 4,000 Muslims in jail versus 300 Hindus and a few more than 300 Sikhs. Now the question I ask is, if all the mosques and the biggest community being Muslims and all the *madrassas* operating every day teaching from 3.00 or 4.00 'til 7.00, and you are producing 4,000 people in the prisons, there is something definitely wrong in the manner of the teaching... What is happening is a kind of dis-syncronisaton, the teaching in a western society is an absolute metropolis of modernity. They are teaching them *taqlid* Islam and I tell them, 'Do yourself a favour, go back home'. It's like the story of the elephant. Everyone has the elephant but someone has his trunk, someone his tail and so on, but you don't have the *gestalt* view of Islam, you have one end of Islam... So

if you are talking about disinformation or misinformation in the host country I am making the assertion that the Muslims themselves in this country are so confused, given the situation of modernity and secularism, and the structure of this civilization, that they are not portraying a picture of Islam which is decreasing that disinformation, if anything they are increasing it.

Raza also called for a change in the attitude of imams:

Many Muslim scholars who have been participating and contributing their views about music, either in favour or against, I doubt that even 10 per cent have personally visited any music classes in schools. We have just made our own assumptions and then we start giving our own opinions. So let us talk to each other, to the people who are involved in this particular branch of education. If we have properly educated, suitably qualified imams in this country I am sure it will be rather easier to accept these challenges and be able to offer a solution of these problems.

The fault should not be attributed to the scholars alone, says Kelani, even though they do not always agree about what is acceptable. She feels that the Muslim people do not know enough about their religion:

Also I say it is the fault not just of the Muslim scholars but of the Muslims themselves because we do not know our religion properly and if we do not know it properly how are we going to tell others about it? Including our religion's relationship to music – we don't know enough about it.

The different ways in which people use vocabulary was a problem in these interviews. As a musician from Western society I use the terms 'sacred' and 'secular' to refer to music written either for use inside or outside the church. The term secular has a different meaning for Muslims. In the West it cannot be assumed that you are a Christian, but if you are born into an Islamic society you are automatically a Muslim. If you live according to the Islamic laws you are a good Muslim; if you do not you are a secular Muslim. Where music is concerned it was suggested that I talk about Islamic, for music associated with worship, and cultural for music that was not.

DH: They also had secular music for ceremonial reasons didn't they?

AH: Yes, but that would come in the frame of cultural music which is not Islamic music. Islamic music would be *qawali* and war music. The war music is such unique music that if you are inspired by it you are really inspired towards martyrdom. Any other music is not Islamic and I say very clearly any other music is cultural music. The word secular has a particular connotation. In the Western context it is used to mean minus religion, not only minus religion but also anti God. You need to say 'religious' or 'non-religious' music.

DH: So, non-religious music?

AH: No, not non-religious but cultural. Cultural music is used in all Muslim countries, in the Indian sub-continent, all the Arab worlds, Africa, everywhere. So if you walk in those countries, live in those countries, as I have, visit Pakistan, you will hear music all around – that's culture. You are not hearing that music and saying I am inspired to follow Islam but it's at the back of your mind. And none of the people will raise any objections to that.

A similar difficulty emerges when considering the terms 'traditional' and 'fundamental'. Because fundamental has connotations of Islamic terrorists and extremists I was encouraged to use the term traditional instead. For many Muslims, however, a fundamentalist is one who is following the fundamentals of the Qur'an, and the term is used in a very constructive way. But Kelani used these terms differently. She talks of 'strict' Muslims and 'traditional' Muslims, and the traditionalists are her 'villains'. She said, 'Traditionalists are the cancer of the Arab and Muslim culture'. She is particularly upset with some traditional Muslims, who uphold many of the rules supposedly mitigating against women, but no longer follow the basic rules of Islam. She objects to Muslim men who have lax sexual mores, drink, do not fast, do not pray or go to the mosque, and then tell her that she is letting Muslims down because she sings. These are the people she called traditionalists. Akhtar agrees with Kelani on this point:

Unfortunately in Islam, as with the other main religions and all cultural societies, the main voices are governed by men. Yes, it seems very much to be a man's world. So the interpretation is done through a man's eyes too. The result of this is that men take advantage and the words 'hypocrisy' and 'double standards' creep in. I have now gone past the stage of anger and frustration when people are ready to condemn the arts for all the vices and refuse to take off the blinkers and look at any of the good points. Yet these very same people are so ready to watch, listen and enjoy the most provocative of films, music and magazines. It's become a joke now.

Music and Muslims

> Islam is not a private thing; it is not a personal thing; it is not a com-
> mercialised thing. Islam is in the public sphere, it is action. (Asaf
> Hussain)

All actions in Islam fall into five categories: compulsory, recommended, allowed/tolerated, disapproved and forbidden. I asked Sr
Ruqaiyyah where she thought that music belonged:

RWM: Music fits into most categories as far as I am concerned. It de-
       pends on what type of music it is and I would say that any
       music which is sexual, nationalistic or sheer show-offy, then
       that is *haram*, forbidden.

DH: Would it not be acceptable if it was Pakistanis being nationalis-
       tic because that is part of the fighting spirit?

RWM: I would say no. That's a perfect example of where Pakistan has
       got its Islam wrong. I don't think there's anything wrong with
       any national anthem – God Save the Queen – but there's every-
       thing wrong with Rule Britannia. There is a difference, and it
       would depend on the wording of your anthem, if your anthem
       is a prayer then that's fine but if it is 'let's do down everyone
       else because they are inferior', then that would be seen as un-
       Islamic. Disapproved would be anything which led towards
       those behaviours, as in Judaism, we have 'hedge', a sort of
       barrier to keep away from anything which is forbidden, so any-
       thing which was suspect would be disapproved. In the tolerated
       bracket would come everything else. All the secular stuff: folk
       songs, classical music, the vast range of what I would call 'real'
       music would be in that section. The vast mass of pop music
       wouldn't be but most of the rest would. Anything which
       actually uplifted the soul, broadened the mind and brought you
       closer to God, would be recommended. I don't know if any
       Muslim would go so far as to say that any music was com-
       pulsory. In some households I've been in watching Hindi films
       they wouldn't listen to the music, they'd flash forward until it
       was finished. So people are struggling to keep the rules as they
       see them: dance sequences and the music were time wasting,
       sexual, blatant so they get them out of the way.

Why music has come to be unacceptable to many Muslims seems an
important question to ask. Ahmed told me why music was originally
banned, which was dependent on the idea of music being bad by
association. He said:

Before Islam, music was used for two purposes: for pleasure and for worship. For worship it was used in the house of God in Ka'bah, where there were 360 idols and they would come and use dancing until the people got into a state of mind whereby they didn't know what they were doing. The rules are called 'sharia' and they are to protect you from others and to protect them from you. So now people do not do things which are offensive to others, like taking their clothes off. And the second reason, in order to have pleasure with their music they used to have alcohol and they got drunk. Through drinking and alcoholism there are lots of tribal wars and fighting. But because music was often associated with alcohol the rule banning music came as well.

I asked Iqbal about this:

DH: Has the word 'music' got undesirable associations?

MI: Yes, connotations and associations. Vocal music is generally acceptable. When it comes to instrumental music if you play to arouse promiscuity and permissiveness then it is definitely for-bidden because anything that leads to sexual laxness is not allowed.

Another reason I have been given for music being unacceptable is linked to the notion that Islam included music when it encouraged Hindus to embrace the faith. Hussain did not agree with this:

DH: One of the things which I find most interesting is that some Muslims have said that because Hindus have so much music in their religion, and because there is this great divide traditionally between Muslims and Hindus, when Islam began in the Asian sub-continent having the music was a way of encouraging Hindus to become Muslims. Therefore the more fundamental Muslims who wanted to go back to what they saw as a purer form of Islam reacted against any music. Is that an argument you've heard?

AH: That is an argument I've heard. But that's not a valid argument. The valid argument would be that any music which is about love, sex, any music which is for belly dancing or titillating your sexual feelings, that is all banned.

The idea of music being banned because of its association came out time and time again. Styer said:

We view the world through associations so we cannot ignore the associations of some things... the elements of music are objective – the frequencies, harmonies and so on – but the conventions which are followed to make happy or sad emotions in Western music are subjective and passed through shared experience or culture. We associate new music with old, forming a large part of our interpretation.

Massaoudi agreed that music performed in the context of loose women and wine would always be *haram*. Music, 'in a disco or club context where the type of music, often unacceptable lyrics, and drinking of alcohol could lead to womanising and possibly adulterous relationships cannot be allowed'. However, Whiteman did not agree with this at all:

> I don't accept that things can be haram by association. This just doesn't stand up to reason. The *hadiths* often quoted by people who are very against music are always the ones which are about a recorded social event of music, drinking, fornicating, whatever, and then you think, hang on, you could ban anything by association. Most things in life can be used for good or ill. Music, drinking and sex can all be used for good or evil.

Hussain also spoke in this vein when he said that something cannot be *haram* in itself, it is the use you put it to that counts. For example you can beat a drum to accompany a belly dancer, which would be *haram*, but you could beat that same drum in a holy war, which would not only be *halal* but also expected of you. Talking of the *hadith* banning music because of its association with women and drink he said, 'It is a very foolish person who takes a *hadith* like that and accepts it totally'. Kelani said:

> In the dawn of Islam , when Muhammad was teaching the new religion, music was banned and I understand why, even as a musician now. In those times it was associated with prostitution and whore houses, it was associated with many things which were anti-female. To be honest it was associated with debauchery with idolatry and rituals.

Professional musicians and, by association, music teachers are often not treated with respect. This is because of music being associated with *haram* activities. I asked Raza about this:

DH: So what would you say to Muslims who use the argument that professional musicians and music teachers are not to be respected?

SR: Perhaps I would be reluctant to agree to that sort of statement. Whether we agree to accept a choice of other people or not, whether we agree with other people or not as long as ways of life are concerned we should appreciate their achievement in their profession and their qualifications. I am also strongly in favour of initiating some sort of review by the Muslim scholars who are based in this country on these issues. I am not in favour of importing all the ideas from abroad for Muslims who live in this country. The situation and the environment is entirely different and the Muslim scholars who have lived in this country they are the competent and suitably qualified scholars to look into these issues and review it. I certainly and naturally will be advocating that sort of approach and reviewing where we start challenging the universally accepted spiritual and moral code of Islam, but within a particular framework of Islamic teachings there is no harm in encouraging that sort of initiation of reviewing those issues here locally.

Hewitt has more negative views about music, which are to some extent in agreement with Lambat, who gave the following as his aims for writing his book:

- to investigate the status of Music with reference to the Qur'an, *Ahadith* and Classical works

- to analyse the Psychological effects of Music

- to analyse the social Impact of Music

- to prescribe recommendations on findings. (Lambat, 1998 p3)

What I find interesting here are Lambat's references to what he calls 'classical works' and his comments on musicians today. For example, his main reason against music is that it is a tool of the devil.

The existence of Evil personified as Satan or the Devil is a widely accepted view. However, it is only Islam which maintains a clear, precise and non-superstitious position on Satan. Music is but one tool that Allah has permitted Iblis (Satan) to utilise in the overall scheme and test of the Earthly Life. (Lambat, 1998, p27)

One of his main issues with modern pop music is the presence of backtracking. This process, he says, is used by the pop industry to control and influence people's minds. It is a system whereby hidden messages are inserted into the songs which are designed to be picked up by the subconscious mind. An example he gave is of the song *Another one bites the dust* by Queen, for which he said the backward lyrics are *It's fun to smoke marijuana*. Lambat concludes his book by saying that it is not just a sin to listen to music yourself but a sin also not to actively try to stop others from performing or listening to it. And so to the punishment:

> When a sin is committed, before an individual or group and they do not stop it, despite the ability, then Allah inflicts a severe punishment before death. (*ibid* p46)

Whether or not musical instruments are permitted is an area I found to have a particular resonance with Muslims. At times the conversations became rather confused: when talking about music, some people meant only singing whilst for others music implied the use of musical instruments.

I discussed with Raza when he thought musical instruments were allowed.

DH: Are there times when you put instruments with the singing?

SR: Yes, all the *qawalis* they are with music [ie musical instruments]. *Qawali* is the singing of religious poetry and there is a tradition of singing as well like poetry in praise of God, or of Prophet Muhammed, peace be upon him, or poems in praise of Sufis. They are sung without music as well but qawali is a sort of singing where music is a must.

DH: Are there musical instruments which are accepted and ones which are not acceptable or could you use any musical instruments that people wanted to play?

SR: In fact there are no very clearly identified musical instruments in the Sufi references. They allow the music, this is the important thing. Of course traditionally the Sufis had been flourishing in the East so Eastern musical instruments have been in extensive use in qawalis. But I'm sure that if we were to witness the Sufis in the West they would have used the Western instruments as well.

In the Sunni school of Islam there is a particular aversion to musical instruments. Akhtar was aware that many people do not accept instruments and when asked her view said, 'To my knowledge they are not accepted'. But she didn't know the reasons for this and found it difficult to understand, 'To me it doesn't seem right because in Arabia they have the flute. The shepherds would go out with their sheep and they'd have a flute'. Raza gave an example of a time when an instrument was used and was not banned by the Prophet.

> There are references in the sayings of the Prophet Muhammad, peace and blessings be upon him, that on one occasion, it was the day of *'Eid*, the day of celebration, and some of the young people they were celebrating it and singing some songs to express their festivity and joy of the occasion, and they were also using at least

one musical instrument, and the objection was raised even at that very time in front of the Prophet, and the Prophet's response was, 'Let them do, it is an occasion of happiness and festivity'.

Trevathan, Head of the Islamia Primary School, said that he was absolutely clear about his feelings on the use of instruments,

I know that it's allowed and it will be and it's part and parcel of human culture and Islamic culture, which is very, very rich and very, very deep and spiritual and it will always have music. They can do what they like but they're not going to suppress that music, or people like me or Abd al-Lateef [Whiteman] or anyone else.

But this does not mean that he has been able to use instruments at his school. Ahmed, the imam at Islamia, said:

This school, Islamia, is unique. The example of this school is an example whereby we are trying to unite the factions who interpret Islam in different ways. Islamia is for everybody. We have all the kind and shade of Shia all the shade of Sunni Muslims together in this school. Therefore everything we try to do has to accommodate everyone, the very, very strict and the very, very liberal. So in that sense I would say that instruments offend lots of people and we should say 'no'. But I can say to them, 'Look, the Prophet allowed the drums to be played', little by little I hope we can bring them to understand the real essence of the teaching of music

I asked Trevathan how he could fulfil all of the National Curriculum requirements without using musical instruments. He replied,

Music generally has been a issue at Islamia, partly because having become a state school we are now expected to fulfil the National Curriculum music requirements.

AT: We've had an Ofsted [Office for Standards in Education] inspection here about a month ago and the person in charge of music came in and said, 'I'm sure you're going to agree with me, music is in a complete mess'. I said, 'You're absolutely right'. Our music teacher was teaching them how to *read* music. It must have been for singing because at the moment we do not teach any instruments whatsoever, and music consists primarily of singing, and the occasional drumbeat.

DH: Two questions follow on from that: one, what sort of music would you like the children to be involved in and two, to what extent do they listen to music in school?

AT: Not much. There are moves in the school, amongst some of the consultants that we have, that in order to fulfill the National

Curriculum children should be familiar with different types of music. Whether or not they play it or listen to it they should be familiar with it.

DH: So how do you get familiar without playing or listening?

AT: Well I don't think they are suggesting that they don't listen but that they listen in class and that's it.

DH: How about in classes other than music, do they do any dance or drama which includes music?

AT: Drama we do, with singing.

DH: And dance? Is it part of PE?

AT: No. We are not fulfilling the National Curriculum.

DH: What is stopping you being able to implement more music and dance?

AT: What's stopping me is the combination of the more vociferous parents, who reflect the fundamentalists – I hate using the word fundamentalist, it's a very misused word – I think you know what I mean by it, and the governors and the trustees.

DH: How do you reflect on the fact that it's not going on?

AT: I've seen similar situations in schools that I taught in before I came back to Islamia...

DH: In this country?

AT: Oh yes, in this borough, Brent. One was in an assembly. I'd just arrived in the school and in assembly the deputy sat down and played the piano as the children filed into the hall. There were two Iraqi girls who stuck their fingers in their ears and sat down and stayed like that throughout the 5 minute period of playing. Then they left the hall still with their fingers in their ears.

I asked Ahmed what sort of music he would like to see the children engaging in at Islamia. His response was:

I believe any music which will uplift, which will teach them good and make people closer, that will show them the glory of the creation and the glory that you can see around us.

Yusuf Islam, formerly Cat Stevens, is the Chair of Governors at Islamia. Twenty years ago, when he embraced Islam, he rejected music entirely, believing that he should concentrate on his religion. It was in this frame of mind that he started Islamia and became a leading figure in the British Muslim community. Gradually he has come to realise that music and Islam are not entirely incompatible, and has begun song-writing again. He said that his wife bought his son a guitar:

> She got him a black Gibson and so we had this instrument sitting around in the house again and it was very difficult for me not to pick it up. (Williamson, 2005, p14)

Having come back to music himself he now feels that all the requirements of the National Curriculum – including music – can be included in the curriculum of Islamia School, and Trevathan is hoping it will begin in September 2005.

Styer said that at Suffah they debated whether it would be acceptable for children before puberty to use musical instruments, but decided against it. He believes that after puberty no Muslim child should play instruments. He quoted a *hadith* which said that string and woodwind instruments are unacceptable. He said:

> The soul is a fine substance which inhabits our mind, which is attracted to types of beauty. Some work with the consciousness of Allah and some work against it. Instruments do not have words so they can be interpreted in any way.

I asked him if he ever played musical instruments and he replied that he does not unless there is a specific need. For example, he cannot sing music by sight and so in order to learn new songs to teach the children, he sometimes has to play the tune on a keyboard to hear how it goes.

According to some people music should not be allowed during Ramadan, the month in the Islamic year when the Prophet received the Qur'an. During this month Muslims spend many hours reading the Qur'an and praying so it may well be that there is no time for music. This is different from banning it and bears no relation to teaching a subject in school time. Ramadan is also the month for rejoicing – which in many cultures means that there is more music. One city where I did research sent out a letter to schools stating that any pupil wishing to withdraw from music lessons during Ramadan should be allowed to, explaining:

> During Ramadan music for Muslims is focused on hearing the recitation of the Qur'an and consequently other music is put to one side. Therefore, please be particularly alert to avoid offending through the use of music in assemblies and on other occasions in the school day.

I have not come across this situation elsewhere and made it the basis for a question to interviewees. Here is a selection of replies:

That situation with Ramadan is absolute nonsense. I'm going to really stick my neck out now but I think that people who are so adverse to music in that fashion are pretty silly. I mean, I could tell you loads of stories but I don't want to. It's a silly, ridiculous position to take and I think, in my opinion, it has no place within the traditional understanding of sound, music, whether or not it's permissible or not. That type of approach is just ridiculous. (Trevathan)

Fasting is very intense and music can sound amazing whilst in the fasting state but in recent times I just like reciting or listening to the Qur'an in that time. Music can intrude. But I've come to that naturally – no-one has forced me to that. You can't impose things like banning music in this society even if you wanted to. How would you do it? Which is why I find all this posturing about music so pointless. (Whiteman)

I've never heard of that at all, all Muslims become a bit more religious in Ramadan, it's inevitable because you are concentrating wholesale on religion. (Sr Ruqaiyyah)

The idea of opting out of music during Ramadan is absurd; there is nothing in the tradition that suggests that should be so. (Styer)

Politics seems to play a part in some of the decisions. It has been suggested to me that the city council made this response for political reasons, possibly to 'hold out an olive branch', and that the response of some local Muslims was also political. For those who oppose music at any time, getting music stopped during Ramadan is a way of banning music for part of the year, even though it cannot be entirely banned in state schools.

In Pakistan much music is objected to on grounds that it is of Indian origin. But the same music was the natural heritage of Pakistan before the country was partitioned. Sometimes it is presented as a Hindu/Muslim problem but, however presented, it is really part of Pakistan's continuing desire to find its own identity, and part of this is a rejection of anything Indian. Massaoudi agreed:

What you experienced in Pakistan you could easily experience in the Arab world. This is what I call reactionary Islam and due to colonisation and due to current political situations, as in the case between Pakistan and India, you find that a number of Muslims have to go through this phase. They can only find themselves in reaction to a system or another culture.

Mrs Akhtar was anxious that her daughter should not answer any questions which might be seen as political. This arose because

Akhtar mentioned how she responded to questions about Salman Rushdie. The conversation went as follows:

DH: It seems to me that that was something political and this is what happens, things become political rather than religious.

Mrs A: Do not say much more about this, it is a political matter.

NA: In the West I am sad to say Islam has definitely been mixed with politics, especially in the present political climate. My mother has always tried to protect me from these kinds of things, in case I am misquoted or misunderstood. or even say the wrong thing.

DH: I wasn't going to ask about Salman Rushdie, I was going to say that I think that some areas with the music are mainly political. There are Muslims who have told me that there are a group of Muslims who want to make a statement. Because they don't teach music in their schools they don't think Muslims should have to do music in a state school. Do you think politics and religion sometimes get confused?

NA: Arts are generally not encouraged because of the historical connection with all the vices that one can think of. Whether they are in the East or West, especially in this day and age, our young Muslim adults need to be more with it in terms of everything from arts to science and religion. Can there not be a good balance?

Mrs A: No, no the music is actually forbidden in Islam. It is really true, especially for girls.

NA: What it says is that the voice of a woman should not be heard outside the four walls of her home.

Mrs A: What does that mean?

NA: But she can sing and welcome. Our Prophet, peace be upon him, as he entered Mecca as he returned, they were singing and clapping and playing the duff. They were singing then and in that procession there must have been loads of men and women. It's very confusing at times and my mother has a point.

Akhtar asked her mother how men and women could give the call to prayer if a woman's voice was not to be heard outside her four walls, a theme I continued.

Mrs A: The purpose of your interview with Najma is to do with whether women in Islam are allowed to sing. *Adzan* is always given by men.

NA: I was in Bosnia just as the war ended and I heard a woman giving the call to prayer and it was beautiful. I was on route to a refugee camp and we stopped at the only Muslim radio station in Bosnia. And guess what, it was run by women. The *adzan* was a recording that was played five times a day. I questioned it at the time as to it being said to be forbidden. The girl simply said, 'Where is it written? This is a hard time here for Muslims, so does it really matter?' People may say 'well a women's voice is too sexy to do the Call,' but hey what planet are they on, because men have very sexy voices too, does not this defeat the purpose here? It again all comes down to the male superiority as to what they consider is, and what is not, allowed.

DH: But generally it's OK for men but not for women?

Mrs A: That's it.

DH: And singing is also OK for men but not women?

Mrs A: Yes.

NA: I don't know.

Mrs A: When Najma was saying that they were singing together when the Prophet, peace be upon him, came to Medina or Mecca I don't know what they are saying, is that music alright but not the other? I don't know.

NA: But that's how it is interpreted. The general consensus is that men can sing but women can't. Is that culture or religion? Referring back to the scene of the return to Mecca, the rejoicing was done or performed by both men and women together. They were singing and dancing together. Voices were in unison as well as solo. It's all a matter of how we as modern day people interpret this. Does that really mean that singing, jumping up and down, which maybe construed as dancing, is forbidden?

I asked Akhtar if she had often come across occasions when it was acceptable for men to sing but not women. She said that she hadn't until recently and that it had come as a surprise to her when she was doing a workshop in a girls' school in East London. She had taken her whole band and played to girls aged 13-17. When she had finished several approached her and said, 'How can you sing? You're a Muslim aren't you?' Akhtar directed them to her mother for a reply. She continued:

So I remember them all clambering around my mother asking how come she allowed me to sing and saying, 'We want to sing but our mothers won't let us, how can we sing?' Really they were just kids and you can't encourage them to do something that would upset their *status quo*... I think Mummy just said that they would need to talk to their parents if they wanted to sing, but that education was the most important thing to concentrate on first, giving my example.

I did not set out to be a singer, it all happened, for want of a better word, so slowly and innocently. One thing gradually led to another and my darling mother has been with me at every step of the way. Travelling and attending almost every single festival and performance I have done. Some people would joke about it, but I took it as a Western attribute that they could not understand the trust and respect that we have for our parents, and that I was so lucky that my mother could be there with me not as a chaperone but as my well wisher and companion.

Sometimes when I see kids, especially young Muslim girls, being suppressed by their environment, not religion, it makes me so sad, because there is so much to see and do in this beautiful world that God has made for us. I have no regrets because of all the wonderful experiences I have had. My life is richer and fuller because of my music. Is that a sin or a blessing?

Kelani and Akhtar both agree that the restrictions have been imposed by their culture and not their religion. Akhtar believes that it will eventually change, but Kelani is less optimistic. Opportunities for women and girls is something I also discussed with Raza:

DH: The girls I was teaching felt unable to express themselves, or even allow themselves to think in that creative, free way. Is that something which is endemic to Islam now? Is it something which music, not just music but many other creative arts, would help?

SR: Yes, definitely, that will help if our young generation is allowed to play an active and free role in the community. I am very optimistic in that respect that as far as the Islamic law is concerned that men and women have been given, by Islam, equal privilege, or equal rights in terms of their intellectual freedom. Unfortunately under some influences of our indigenous societies that freedom of education and intellect has been not been coming through so profoundly, but here we have got an opportunity and we need to explore that.

The Islamic view about music as a profession was discussed in Chapter 2. It is interesting to hear how these two Muslim women musicians fared. Akhtar's mother worried that her daughter would not be able to get married because no one would marry a woman musician. Already in her late twenties, old for a Muslim woman still to be single, Akhtar is unconcerned:

> That's wrong; there are many people who would marry me, but you know it's the chance for me to have performed all over the world and to have travelled. I could be married with three kids and not have seen any of the world. Through my parents being open-minded about what I wanted to do I have had these chances. I have truly been very lucky, because to achieve all the things that I have, all the travelling, seeing the world, meeting people from so many different walks of life and actually being invited with my band to perform for the Palestinian people, and having the courage to go to Bosnia, were all just a huge eye opener for me. I could never have imagined what the reality of these type of situations really were, except to only see what the media portrays in the west.

Kelani is happily married to an English Muslim but she has suffered because of making music her profession.

> Until I decided to become a professional singer there was never a considerable conflict. There's never been a conflict and my parents are very much practising Muslims. In fact they'd spent a lot of their money and time on getting a teacher to teach me classical piano. It was their pride and joy. My father listened to George Gershwin, to Irving Berlin, to classical music, to Egyptian music and to the Qur'an, because my father is the son of a Sheikh. I grew up in a house which had pictures of grandfathers and uncles wearing turbans but it never clashed with me listening to a Gershwin song. They weren't very happy with me doing cabaret style numbers and imitating Lisa Minelli and doing *New York, New York*. My father was a bit quiet when I was doing the Palestinian things because it is a national duty, what really drove them up the wall were the jazz songs, the standards, the show stoppers – they just couldn't cope with them... and it's been a volcano with my parents ever since.

Interestingly, playing the piano was acceptable, although not as a profession. But singing was always a problem. Kelani has a theory that it is because Arab singing is produced through the diaphragm and the body rather than the head, as in Western classical singing. She thinks that because it is not head resonance but use of the body that it appears to be more sexual.

> The reason I'm telling you this is because there is a cousin of mine who is not a real strict Muslim but a traditionalist who told me that if only I'd continued with the piano they'd have supported me all the way through, but not singing. He told me in this room and I was shocked when he said this.

Political influences also come into play: when she gives concerts of Palestinian folkloric songs in Palestine and Lebanon, women with their heads covered, and strict men attend and love it. But they would not let their own daughters perform.

Fifteen years on, her parents have accepted that Kelani is a successful musician and are proud of what she does.

DH: Have they come to hear you sing?

RK: Here, no, but in Kuwait they have. There was always the pride and the grin. I remember a famous concert I gave in 1988, when I was still a practising biologist, it was a hard concert. It was during the Palestinian uprising so it was a fund raising concert, their support was phenomenal. I don't like to tell you 100% black or 100% white, I must tell you the truth. I remember my father lost his mother one week before the concert so normally in the Middle East mourning is mourning, no singing, no music, and the classic thing was it was during the holy month of Ramadan. Every day after having the *iftar*, the meal of breaking the fast at sunset, my father would receive the people who came to pay their condolences. After they had left he would roll up the carpets and say, 'Come on Reem, start rehearsing with your folk dancers'.

DH: So it's alright to raise money from performing for the Palestinian cause but you can't earn a living from performing?

RK: Absolutely. There is a Hamas pop group in Gaza, it's only men and only with a drum kit and only Islamic songs. In fact they remove the lyrics from the secular, traditional songs and plug them in with religious ones instead.

DH: Now that there's not the same sort of pressure, the traditionalists don't want you to sing any more?

RK: No, what I'm saying is now in Palestine the scene is not encouraged as it was in the intifada, but in my case I have chosen a course which is still acceptable but still not with strict Muslims. The simple example is the refugee camps in Lebanon. Whenever I go there, to concerts to sing Palestinian folkloric song, they love it. Including women who are scarved, including very strict men. They still come and they love it. But they wouldn't let their daughters do it.

DH: And they wouldn't come if you were doing more the jazz type?

RK: That's coming to the point. I was invited by a jazz festival in Beirut to perform and my supporters in the camps went mad. 'How could you, Reem, how could you?' And I told them, 'Jazz started through suffering, jazz and blues, OK, not carbaret style, but a lot of what I am doing now, a lot of the jazz is the black African way of singing the way you sing'. What the Hamas pop band do in Gaza is considered complete blasphemy by Taliban standards so you even have a hierarchy of things.

An article by Hudson (*Guardian*, 1995), confirmed this.

> The rhythms are traditionally Arab, the loose structure Western rap, and the combination is underpinned by blood-curdling lyrics about jihad, holy war. The songs of Islamic fundamentalist groups like the *Shehadin* (Martyrs) are propelling Hamas rock to the top of the Palestinian charts.

However, in a second interview with Kelani in 2005, she told me that music in Palestine is no longer seen as acceptable by many of Hamas, although they are not saying it is music itself that they disapprove of.

> When we met before it was at the beginning of the second intifada and things have moved on now. In the last five years Hamas has gained control, and more popularity, and in many cases it is because it does not have corruption, it has to be said, as opposed to many of the apparatuses of the Palestinian authority. Hamas doesn't have that. They are hard working but it's not just a liberation movement, they want to make an Islamic state. Hamas is actually cancelling gigs now. It seems that in every principality where they are gaining control they are beginning to cancel concerts of Palestinian music. There was a time when it was Israel that used to cancel these concerts. Palestinians used to go to these gigs as a form of defiance.

A Hamas led council in the West Bank has now banned outdoor music and dance performances (BBC 1/7/05 news website). A council spokesman for the town of Qalqilya is reported to have said, 'the council had been elected to protect the conservative values of the city, which included not approving of men and women mixing'. Reportedly, a West Bank concert ended in chaos five days later, when dozens of gunmen disrupted a concert, 'This is not the time to have parties like this in Nablus', one of the masked gunmen was quoted as saying. Kelani observed:

But what more and more people are admitting now within Hamas is that they think it is wrong to have music in Islam and that's why they don't want it. They are even banning concerts that are seen as an act of defiance.

Palestinian singer Rim Banna has been quoted as saying: 'I feel more like a fighter than a musician' (*Haaretz*, 2005):

I have always expressed the Palestinian voice and sung political songs. I grew up in that kind of home, with a mother who always fought against discrimination and for human rights; but the art was not art under fire. I could devote myself more to purely musical thought. I could appear at Palestinian festivals as much as I wanted, in relative security, and concentrate on creating a Palestinian style that would be both original and genuine, and also personal and my own... Everything happened with such great rapidity, greater than I could manage to follow. Suddenly people were falling victim, and tanks began to shoot, and bombardments, and blood. I couldn't understand – are we really here, or maybe in Afghanistan? As a Palestinian woman, I had to do something concrete to help my people, to come myself and support them – and I knew that I had to travel and perform in cities in the West Bank despite the difficulty and the danger, that I mustn't stop, and that despite the roadblocks and the soldiers, the music would continue to be heard. In this way music became my weapon; unfortunately I need to use military images like 'fighter' and weapon,' but isn't this what we are seeing around us all the time?

Who her audiences are is an important consideration for Akhtar. She has not sung in Asian countries but when she performs to predominantly Muslim Asian communities in the North of England she is more careful about her dress and dance movements than when in London and the South. She said she was baffled to see a row of religious men with beards, turbans and distinctive coats sitting at the front at one concert. She had been warned that they would be there but could not understand why they had come. If they were so religious what were they doing there? At another concert in the north, the audience were segregated, with the men downstairs and the women upstairs. She told me:

I didn't like that. But there were some rebellious girls, really nice girls so I don't really like to say rebellious, and they were sitting upstairs and I was focusing all my attention upstairs. I wasn't looking down at all. Eventually, after the interval, half of them came down and sat right under my nose and again I focused all my attention on them.

Kelani told me:

> There isn't one thing that the Muslim scholars have agreed upon with regard to music, nothing that the Arabs have agreed upon, nothing that the traditionalists have agreed upon or the Palestinians or even the Muslims themselves, not just their scholars.

Akhtar and Kelani have different views about performing in venues where alcohol is consumed. Akhtar was asked to sing at the Glastonbury Festival and initially encountered resistance from her parents.

> Coming from an Asian family, whether Muslim or Hindu, performing at pop festivals is like performing in a club. The moment you say festival they say, 'drugs' and all the other vices, and a club is always portrayed in Indian films as a very bad place.

She overcame the resistance, performed at Glastonbury, with her parents present, and was subsequently invited to Ronnie Scott's club in London. Her parents were persuaded to let her perform when they heard that it was not just any club but a very famous jazz venue with a good reputation. Kelani has also been invited to perform at Ronnie Scott's but has so far refused. She said:

> I still don't go to gigs because I'm not comfortable singing in pubs where there is alcohol, and this is actually hindering my career because I will not even sing in Ronnie Scott's. I am from the Kelani family and my grandfather lying in his grave and his grand daughter singing in a nightclub. But again, if you are a jazz musician it is a very respectable place. I might end up doing it [singing at Ronnie Scott's or somewhere similar] but I will feel uncomfortable with it, probably I always will be uncomfortable with it. It's to do with upbringing. My mother-in-law, who is English, told me that her mother would not have let her sing in a place like Ronnie Scott's 50 years ago. So it's not just Islam, it's basic human values. Some of the things my English mother-in-law talks about are similar to what my mother talks about.

Many of the disadvantages Muslim women currently suffer are no different to those that women experienced in the UK in the past. Remember the music hall song, *Don't put your daughter on the stage, Mrs Worthington*, which suggests that acting is not a suitable career for a girl? My mother, from a Cornish, Methodist farming family, once told me that she felt uncomfortable doing dancing at school because she knew her mother disapproved of it.

Although Mrs Akhtar allows her daughter to earn a living as a professional singer, she nevertheless maintains that it is *haram*. This conversation took place between mother and daughter:

DH: Do you see any difference between earning a living from music and just enjoying music in any other realm?

NA: Well, I don't think there is anything bad because I think I am also giving people a lot of pleasure. God has given me a gift and the gift is my voice. If I can use my voice to give people pleasure, as well as God...

Mrs A: That is the thing. Giving pleasure and earning the money giving pleasure it is *haram*. That's what...

NA: No, but if you are a doctor and you are curing somebody and you really enjoy helping people...

Mrs A: That is a different type of...

NA: OK, if you are an architect, you are an artist creating a building that people go and see. The Taj Mahal for example...

Mrs A: (unable to translate)

NA: Why not? You can be intoxicated by looking at a building.

Mrs A: Not in the same way as by your singing.

NA: No, I disagree. My mother is saying that you cannot be intoxicated by looking at a building. Everybody's different though.

Mrs A: No darling, that is...

NA: People are intoxicated by looking at Stonehenge. They go, 'Wow, this is amazing', they go round and round it.

Mrs A: That is not what I am saying. They say things like if you drink alcohol and the music they are very similar things. The building and Stonehenge they are totally different. The pleasure you get from them is different from the pleasure you get from singing, or you are drinking, or you are dancing.

This lead directly to the question of intoxication, which is bound up with emotion. Emotion is a problem for many Muslims and music is necessarily bound up with emotion. Hewitt said:

I think that music can no doubt stir the soul and emotions, that's what it's for. If it doesn't do that the composer hasn't done his job properly. So the dividing line between the good music and the not so good music and the dangerous music, well, where do you draw that line? And I think it would be very difficult for me to be listening to say, *Academic Festival Overture*, I like overtures, and then my kids come along and they want to listen to Spice Girls, or whatever's there at the moment, and how can I say, you can't listen to that but

I can listen to this? The line has to be drawn somewhere and I think the bad outweighs the good.

Whiteman agrees to a limited extent. He feels that if people cannot tell the difference between good music and bad they should maybe refrain from listening to any. But unlike Hewitt, who believes it could be dangerous to 'stir the soul and emotions', Whiteman believes that emotions, or as he called it in the next quote, ecstasy, are key to life, particularly for Sufis.

> Of course the Sufis have used music traditionally, with and without the use of instruments, for inducing ecstasy and love of God. *Ilm al-tasawuf* (Sufism) is the science of the states of the heart and is one of the fundamentals of Islam, according to Ash'ari, and not an innovation. States of ecstasy come under that category. It concerns its purification, its correction and its illumination.

Abu Hamid al-Ghazzali (1058-1111), a teacher, theologian, religious reformer and mystic wrote *Ihya' 'ulum al-din* (The Revival of Religious Sciences), in which he attempted to integrate Sufism with more orthodox Sunni Islam. Shiloah (1995 p43), wrote of this,

> A major point in his argumentation is the idea that music and singing are means of evoking what is truly in one's heart; under their influence the heart reveals itself and its contents.

Whiteman went on:

> There are sects who hide or deny this aspect of Islam even though it has been a major part of traditional Islam from the time of Junayd and is embedded in the source teaching of our Prophet. It frightens people because they are afraid to look into their hearts for fear of what they might find there. But actually once purified the heart is pure light and ecstasy. Furthermore ecstasy is allied in some way to love. Music is also connected to love and therefore to ecstasy. If that dimension is missing from your life then you're missing something important, something healing and restoring. It's a short step from that to an Islam, to a life, which is just legalistic, dry and tasteless... I want an intelligent and informed debate about music and not just a lot of *hadith* quoting. That is an intellectual betrayal. God has given us minds and intellects to reason. If music was this big evil in our lives then certainly the Qur'an would be reminding us of this on every page but it doesn't. In fact it is not mentioned specifically at all. There are many areas of life where we have to reason things out and where no religious position exists. Allah intended this. This doesn't mean to say there aren't dangers from music, of course there are. But to avoid understanding and teaching music is like the

ostrich advising its young to stick their heads in the sand because the hunters approaching across the sand will then disappear.

As I believe that music is such a large feature of European culture it is almost obligatory that one should learn about it and understand it. Central to the understanding of this is *niyyat* [intention], not rules imposed from a superficial understanding of Qur'an and *ahadith*, that must decide the framework in which music is practiced and studied in this nascent Islamic culture. Rather than burying heads in the sand forbidding the use of music (an impossible task anyway), the new Muslims of the West should extend their knowledge of music generally and especially in the traditional Islamic applications of music and create a new *sphere* of music which encompasses a music for inspiration, teaching, *da'wa*, enjoyment, praise and cele-bration, as well as its known uses in medical therapy and military strategy as practised by the Ottomans and the Andalusian civiliza-tions.

Sr Ruqaiyyah, too, was aware that 'music which draws you out of yourself emotionally can be dangerous because it opens you up to all sorts of influences'. And Trevathan said:

I think it's also important to say that we must tolerate people who have fears about the effects of music and, there's no doubt about it, there is music out there which is counter to the spiritual state.

A salient point in Styer's philosophy is that the person singing should be spiritual himself. He said it is necessary for the singer to be spiri-tual in order to appreciate the beauty and pass it on.

In my conversation with Iqbal I suggested that instrumental music might be less of a risk than music with words which could lead people astray:

DH: Could we come back to the question of musical instruments. If you have instrumental music you do not have words, so they can't be encouraging you in any way of life; there are no words to suggest behaviour.

MI: Music does not need words to excite passions.

DH: So if you have the right words it will take the mind away from the emotions of the music?

MI: The music has a wider range of expression than the words. The way the music has suggestive undertones, there is no clear cut line saying 'this is good' or 'this is bad'. From the most corrupt-ing to the most acceptable is one line.

DH: You don't know what is happening in any one person's mind – what emotions are being created from any piece of music. Doesn't this allow for possible problems?

MI: There are people in other religions who have similar concerns about the corrupting nature of music, particularly pop music. The Muslim community have many worries and they want to hang on to their culture, so these things become more problematic than they are in their own countries.

DH: That's one of the things I wanted to ask, it really touches on two things: one, the idea of people living in a time warp, they go back to families in Pakistan and say it seems much freer. It seems to be to do with preserving the culture as it was when they were there.

MI: They allow much more in their own countries because they know that after that allowance there isn't much danger but here any sort of music could lead you to a problem.

Also linked with intoxication is the Sufi state of *wajd* or trance. Raza said the complete mental state of *wajd* is not common, and not something he has experienced. He describes it as follows:

SR: This is a particular stage of meditation and absorption practised and observed by Sufis and it is a state where a Sufi witnesses the radiant reflection of God's attributes. My feeling would be that when you go into this different world your thoughts, if there are thoughts in that world, would not be bad if in your normal life they are not bad. So I can't see that something terribly bad could happen during that time.

DH: But that is an argument against it.

SR: Yes, but they need to offer certain definite examples for that. It is only a theoretical argument that it might happen. As far as I know, and I have extensively studied lives and thoughts of Sufis, it has never occurred to me, anywhere, in any of these examples, that the Sufis, when they achieve this state of trance are harming anybody or harming themselves or disturbing the normal way of life in their own surroundings.

As a Sufi he believes that the Prophet spent much of the month when he received the Qur'an from Allah in meditation, or trance. Hewitt accepts this might have been the case but since the Prophet is an exceptional human being it would not be bad. For everyone else it is *haram*:

IH: Sufism, again, I find is one of those things where there is no evidence of the Prophet, peace be upon him, or any of his companions doing the things which Sufis say we should be doing to increase our spiritual awareness. And the idea of getting into a trance-like state is a very dangerous state of mind, because you are not aware of what you're saying, what you're doing or where you are. I think that is not what Islam is all about.

DH: So do you think people in that trance-like state would do something that was bad that they wouldn't normally do when they were not in that state?

IH: The possibilities are there that that could be so.

For me music has always been intimately bound with creativity in all its aspects. It therefore seems appropriate to ask about ways in which creativity can be encouraged in Muslim children in whatever form. In interviewing Hussain, I realised that many Muslims were also coming to realise that something was lacking in the education of their children, although they might not acknowledge it. He said:

> This is the problem which came up in a lecture I gave the other day. A girl stood up and stunned the rest of the audience. She asked, Why is it that those who do not believe in a God, who are totally secular, can produce great things and we cannot? Is something wrong with us? And if there is something wrong with us and we claim to be Muslims is there something wrong in Islam?

Ahmed explained why music is a necessary condition of life for him. He said that even before a baby is born it can hear and it listens but that the pleasure we get from listening is not for our body but for our spirit or soul. He said that in order for our body and soul to be together we need desires and it is how a Muslim responds to desires that determines whether he is successful or not. He continued:

> The person who allows his desire to carry on demanding will bring trouble to him or to others. The person who manages to restrain himself and discipline himself, through the rules that the Qur'an lays down, will succeed. So in that sense music is something which could mislead you or lead you. Be moderate. Music, if used in the right way is uplifting...It is very powerful, it makes you want to fly, the soul enjoys it. At the end of the day we say that the music you use should uplift you and bring the goodness out of you. It will make you a better person. But if it brings you to a level where you misuse what you have been given or you enter into a forbidden domain then we say keep away.

Raza and I had the following conversation:

SR: Maybe Islam, as it's being presented, almost inhibits that sort of free thought.

DH: Certainly many of the girls I was teaching felt unable to express themselves or even allow themselves to think in that creative, free way. Is that something which is endemic to Islam now? Is it something which music, not just music but many other creative arts, would help?

SR: Yes, definitely, that will help if our young generation is allowed to play an active and free role in the community. I am very optimistic in that respect that, as far as the Islamic law is concerned, men and women have been given by Islam equal privilege or equal rights in terms of their intellectual freedom.

Hewitt is less interested in the idea of creativity, believing that 'art for art's sake is a very dangerous thing because it corrupts values'. He admits that he was never any good at art at school and says that in that sense, 'creativity is not important and there is the danger of drawing people away from reality'. Although he feels that creativity is not important he does believe that people should be encouraged to think and reason for themselves. He says the situation at present is that 'the average Muslim not only doesn't think, but doesn't think thinking is necessary'. He continued:

> Part of this is down to the control of the information that the people are given by the scholars. Islamic scholarship has stagnated and we need to come back to the idea of developing a culture for Europe, revising our ways but not adopting un-Islamic ways. The elders are still controlling the mosques and creating a time warp, trying to have a little Malawi, little Pakistan, wherever, and that is very dangerous in terms of establishing a Muslim community here as part of this community.

> But we're not conditioned to question the imams. Questioning is seen to be threatening. So when they tell me something I say, 'why?', and they say, 'Why are you questioning me?' I just want them to explain their decisions, not because I'm trying to make them look foolish or trying to overturn it, I just want to know how the decision has been reached to boost my own knowledge. That way of thinking is not part and parcel of the village culture type imam. Some of us in the Muslim schools are trying to create a generation of young Muslims who are confident in their Islam but are also confident to be able to deal with whatever this world throws at them.

The theme of the Islamic faith being in crisis seemed to run through most of the interviews. Hussain told me that if you are a Muslim you need *iman*, knowledge, and *alal*, action, and the two go together. He talked of the medieval state of Islam where many works of art were created and asked 'But where have they gone?' Trevathan took up this cry:

> We do not know who created the Alhambra and the mosaic and cupola work, it was just done. That makes it doubly interesting; it was not individualised, it was just pure, creative expression. And now we are living in a very barren, sterile psyche in the Muslim world. It's not there; what is produced is very stilted and imitative. We've got some people who do these songs, devotional stuff which is a kind of Cliff Richards music, it's just trite and nonsensical. With a few individuals, Abd al-Lateef, and to be honest Yusef Islam, doing some great work in music, we've got this strange dichotomy and it's the Muslim world getting to grips with itself. It's been asleep for 600 years and it's woken up but what has happened in waking up is that it's gone all the way over to one extreme. Hopefully it will slowly begin to balance itself out.

But Ahmed was not sure that creativity could be taught – 'when poets write poetry it is by inspiration'. I replied that although I agreed not everyone could be inspired to write great poetry I did feel it was important to encourage the creative part of every child. He said:

> What I am saying is that... there are some people who write wonderful words and it is a powerful tool for inspiring people, encouraging people, it is very moving. Music helps in that.

Massaoudi talked about the primary school music curriculum she has written which she believes would be acceptable to most Muslims. I asked her about the creative content of it. She showed me that every chapter has a section of suggested activities at the end which contains a list of ideas to promote creativity, such as illustrating a storm using musical instruments. This is exactly the sort of activity found in the National Curriculum. At the time I talked to her, no other Muslim schools were using Massaoudi's curriculum, and even her school has not implemented it, but there has been interest from other countries. At a conference in Cape Town it was mentioned and since then a headmaster has been in touch and is hoping to implement her scheme.

This section concludes with the views of three white Muslim men who all embraced Islam in their twenties. Not all approached music differently when they became Muslims but it manifested itself in a variety of ways. Hewitt was a trombonist playing in an army band in London when he became a Muslim. He began to feel uncomfortable playing in clubs, pubs and even the mess hall because he said it was dominated by alcohol. As he began to find out more about music and Islam he came to the conclusion that all music should be banned.

IH: It's regarded as a grey area although I tend to think it's a very dark grey area although general opinion, I think, would say it's a grey area. I think now when we think about music we think about the rock and roll syndrome and it's the sex, drugs and rock 'n' roll which sticks in people's mind and that's what people fear in the community. I think there is a demonic background behind music, whether people know it or not, I think it's there.

DH: Is that just in the sex, drugs, rock 'n' roll scene?

IH: No, no. I mean we could look at things like *The Magic Flute* and the link with the Freemasons.

For Trevathan musical activity dwindled when he became a Muslim but not because he considered it all to be bad. Partly he lost interest, but also he was aware of Imam Gazali's ruling that response to music was dependent on the time you spent on it, the companions you made music with, and the place you were in. He says his interest in music has now completely returned, which he attributes to 'maturity and seasoned appreciation'.

Whiteman's experience was totally different. At the time, he was singing in a rock band and this he continued to do. He found that it was difficult to maintain an Islamic lifestyle as a rock musician, mainly because of the need to pray five times a day. He eventually left the band, but not for theological reasons. He comes from a Quaker background and for him music was always a spiritual path. He said:

And so it was after coming to Islam in many ways. Music unlocks things in the heart and opens doors, as did calligraphy and architecture for me, but in a very different way. Islamic culture was a revelation to me as it was much more unified and subtle than anything I had experienced hitherto. The recitation of the Qur'an, the singing and the music were closely linked to the calligraphy which recorded it and the architecture in which it was performed. Most of all it was inspiring, which the music of the early 1970s was not. Although Islam was a big change in my life, essentially I am still the same man I was, and whilst it cured me of many things and altered my perception of existence, my passions for beauty in music, design and architecture are now greater than ever.

4

Music and music education
in Muslim countries

Pakistan

Pakistan has an estimated literacy rate of 43.2 per cent (UNESCO, 2002), one of the lowest in the world, and has been drafting various education policies to address this issue for many years. In 1998 the New National Education Policy 1998-2010 pledged to double the literacy rate and universalise primary education, but by 2001 it was still only spending 2.3 per cent of the GNP on education (Ahsan, 2003). The majority of children from middle and upper class families in Pakistan attend private schools. In order to deal with the challenge to increase the literacy rate and achieve primary education for all, Pakistan realised it needed to make use of both the formal and informal education sectors in order to open access to education for the children of poorer families.

In utilising the informal sector Pakistan is acknowledging that the *madrassas*, the Islamic religious schools, can help increase the literacy rate. In the current political climate, the USA in particular is unhappy about more money being put into these schools. Partly as a counter to this initiative, in July 2002 the US Secretary of State announced support for Pakistan's formal education sector. It came in the form of $100 million from the US Agency for International Development to reinforce Pakistan's education reforms over five years. The US had a clear agenda in doing this, support in return for its anti-terrorism campaign being one requirement.

Five days after the military coup of 11 October 1999 I visited Pakistan with my 16 year old daughter, Rachel. I was unsure of what to expect, particularly having landed briefly in Bahrain, where a man was playing a grand piano in the airport to entertain the travellers. While we were waiting for our plane, he played music from the Arab world which sounded lovely to us, themes from James Bond movies, which we found so out of context as to be amusing, and Beethoven's *Moonlight Sonata* – badly. Although this music was probably aimed at a Western audience, it was Muslims who were in most of the seats surrounding the piano. Although most of the Muslims were men there were a couple of women, in headscarves, accompanied by men. This suggests that live music is more widely available in public places in Muslim countries than I had been led to believe, and also that there is an appetite for listening to music, since these people had chosen to listen rather than to sit in the many other seats available in the airport.

We arrived at 7a.m. at the tiny airport in Peshawar, and a greater culture shock would have been difficult to believe. In fact nothing in any Muslim country has ever diminished this first arrival in Pakistan.

The 'taxi' that took us to our hotel

Peshawar is in the North West of the country, right on the border with Afghanistan, and is by far the most traditional area that we were to encounter. As anyone who has done research will know, field work never goes quite as planned. My original intention at the time of booking the trip was to stay with a family in Peshawar but this fell through. While I was there I was also going to visit a school and meet Nazir Azam Sahibzada, who is the Peshawar representative for LAPIS (Luton and Peshawar Initiative for Sustainability). Before I left for Pakistan I found out that the people I had been expecting to meet were not going to be there – they had come to England! As luck would have it Sahibzada and three teachers from Peshawar came to Luton just after I got back from Pakistan. This section is from my conversation with them because it would naturally have fitted in here had it happened in Peshawar.

The three teachers all teach at independent junior schools where music and drama are performed on special occasions. Shazeen Khan is the head of the junior section of a school in Peshawar. Musical instruments were the first subject we discussed. Khan said that the only instrument acceptable for a woman is a drum called a pitcher, a clay pot with a skin across the top, which a bride plays with her ring finger. I mentioned the harmonium but she said that in Peshawar no woman would play a harmonium because it is a Hindu instrument. Women are allowed to sing and dance but not with men. The same is true for men but, strangely, a bridegroom was expected to dance for the women at his wedding.

The situation with the harmonium is interesting. It appears that this instrument is not being played by Muslims in Peshawar because of its association with a different religion. However, it is often difficult in cases like this to know if this is actually anything to do with religion or because of cultural/national differences. This idea may have originated from Pakistan's desire to establish its own identity since its separation from India. Sahibzada thought that music that could be linked to Hinduism was often thought inappropriate for Muslims. For example, some people reject *qawalis*, the Islamic equivalent of hymns, because they came into Islam from the influence of *bhajans* in Hinduism. One explanation given to me for this is that originally Muslims did not have music in their religion. This changed when the Moguls came to India and tried to convert the Hindus. Hinduism is a much more lively religion than Islam, and it was thought necessary to have music to attract the Hindus to Islam.

Unlike some of the Muslims I talked to, Sahibzada is very knowledgeable about Islam and has studied many aspects of it. He said that music is quite acceptable during *Ramadan* because this is a time of rejoicing. However, because there are set readings for each day, with eating and sleeping having to be fitted into the hours of darkness, there is often no time for music. He thought it was probably unacceptable during *Muharram*, the month the Prophet died. The Sunnis commemorate his death for ten days, but for the Shias this is extended to forty days. I followed up on the idea of not having music during *Muharram* in many of my interviews but no one else seemed to think it important. However, it was something that I encountered once during my teaching in Luton. The pupil did not ask to be excused from class music but was not allowed to attend her oboe lessons or orchestra during the forty days.

All four Pakistanis said that it is a question of respect that men and women, even of the same family, do not watch Hindi films together. Even a teenage brother and sister would not watch television or listen to music together. Nazir said the question of respect was to do with culture and not religion: a Muslim may fail to pray five times a day but would still not watch television with women or smoke in front of them. I asked the men if they would watch women dancing if it was not women from their own family where their honour was at stake. They said they would like to see dancing but there was nowhere acceptable for them to see it; the only places where women would dance in front of men were unacceptable for respectable men. Shazeen was very shocked by the idea that they would want to watch women dancing. Most of the women I encountered in Pakistan would have responded to this suggestion in the same way but people in Peshawar held more restricted views than in other areas of Pakistan. They implied that this was because of their proximity to the Afghan border, and the number of Afghans they have living there. Most of the Afghans were refugees from the war and many were Taliban sympathisers, a particularly extreme form of Islam.

On our first day in Peshawar Rachel and I were invited to supper at the home of two brothers who owned a shop near to our hotel. The Butt family came originally from Punjab. 'Jimmy', a psychology graduate and youngest brother, was not married and still lived in the family home. He said he liked all kinds of music and that when he has daughters will let them play instruments. He said you should only believe what it says in the *Qur'an* and not the *ahadith*. He called himself a liberal and thought any music was acceptable as long as neither the performers nor the listeners were having bad thoughts while playing or listening that could lead to bad actions. Although he appeared to be liberal, it was less evident when he talked about other Muslims: he said that Shias are always miserable and Sufis disgusting! He thought that most Pakistani Muslims would respond to the *qawali* of Nusrat Fateh Ali Khan, who is considered to be the greatest exponent of *qawali* on commercial recordings. Khan died in 1997 but because he is so venerated there is no natural successor.

Jimmy's views on music are typical of more liberal Muslims: it is not music itself but its associations which are the problem. His suggestion that it is the *Qur'an* that should be taken note of and that one should be more careful about accepting what is written in the *ahadith* is a view that I heard frequently. His ideas about Shias and Sufis appear to come from a more emotional standpoint. The ways in which some Muslims talk about sects within Islam are often heated, and it reminds me of the relationship between some Protestants and Catholics in Ireland.

Tahira, the 18 year old daughter of the family, did not eat with us but talked to us before supper and listened to the conversation over supper. She said that she would not want to play an instrument or sing, but was vague as to whether this was lack of interest or that she thought it was wrong. When there are men present, it can be difficult to gauge what women really think but she did seem very definite about her views on education: women should be educated to degree standard then marry and have children; there was no intention ever to work. When I asked what the point of the education was she didn't have an answer. In the *Qur'an* it states that women are entitled to the same education as men so they can educate their children.

On our arrival in Lahore we headed for the Al-Hambra Arts Centre which is a beautiful new building. We were disappointed to find that there was no information about what was being performed. There were four art galleries, which appeared to be open, but there was no one in the entrance to any of them. A music block was open but also appeared empty. The administration block was similarly deserted. There were two theatres where we did find some activity, but no one spoke English so we could not communicate. We eventually found someone who was moving furniture who said there was nothing for us to see because the plays were in Urdu and there was no music that week. There was no mention of dance.

At the end of our time in Pakistan I was given the name of Hayat Ahmad Khan, the president of the All Pakistan Music Conference, and I contacted him when I returned to England. If only I'd known about this society before we went we could have gone to as much

A music classroom in an independent school in Lahore, Pakistan

music as we wanted in Lahore that week. The Conference was holding its celebration for 40 years' existence and there were festivities for five of the days we were there. The main events were held at an open air theatre on the outskirts of Lahore and from the programme it was clear that many women musicians were performing. According to Mr Khan, the concerts were sold out but he would have been able to get us in as 'special guests'.

While in Lahore I visited an independent school, one of twelve Beaconhouse schools there. This was a school for boys aged 7-18. The music room was just big enough to squeeze in about 25 boys.

Mr Hamal, the music teacher, was an Evangelical Christian; he played in a group which travelled round Pakistan spreading the word. Much of the music he taught was Westernised or, perhaps more to the point, Easternised Western music. The classes sang with great gusto and appeared to be enjoying themselves. It was really more shouting than singing, so when I heard that the school had a choir I asked if any of the class of 9-10 year old boys were in it. Four from the choir then sang – they obviously loved singing but pitch was not considered important. The songs were usually accompanied by an electronic keyboard rather than a harmonium, but when I expressed interest in hearing the more traditional instrument they found a very dusty and out of tune harmonium to sing to. The choir in the middle school was brought together for special occasions and sang the National Anthem and other patriotic songs. There was an inter-school singing competition which Beaconhouse had won that year.

As well as singing, Mr Hamal gave 'lectures' about music and musical instruments but these did not appear to include listening to music. The boys said at home they liked to listen to Western pop music, particularly Boyzone and Back Street Boys, also one Pakistani group whose name I didn't recognise. Some of them played guitar and keyboard at home. Mr Hamal said they used to use tuned and un-tuned percussion instruments but they no longer use them since the introduction of the keyboard. So the boys do not play any instruments in school because there was only one keyboard. At no time did Mr Hamal mention that there was music he could not teach because they were Muslims. One boy, who played a bit at home, came out to play something to me but the other boys talked throughout it. At the time I did not think much about the question of discipline and respect for education, but it appeared that they did not value music lessons. The boys particularly liked singing *I love to go a-wandering* to a new tune composed by Mr Hamal. When I asked whether the boys did any composition he said they did, but I soon realised that he did not mean composing music but just words to go to music already written. It was noticeable that most of the music I heard while I was in Pakistan was in common time, certainly in the schools.

Wasif Shatique, an 11 year old boy, had come second in the ghazal section of the All Pakistan Music Conference the previous night. His 17 year old brother is also a singer and they are encouraged by their family to have singing lessons even though there is no tradition of music in their family. This is unusual because most musicians follow in a family tradition. His brother was apparently very good but I could not hear him because he was in classes studying for A-levels. Wasif had only had lessons for two and a half months but showed talent. I was surprised that he had come second in an all-Pakistan competition, and asked about entry numbers. There are regional competitions and the best go through but I got the impression that numbers are not high.

A shop selling musical instruments in the bazaar in Lahore, Pakistan

Instruments for show in the Avari

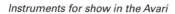

On several days in Lahore we went to the Avari Hotel for lunch, because they did an excellent buffet at which you could have as much of as you liked for the equivalent of £1.50! The Avari is one of the best hotels in Lahore and they play tapes of popular Western classics. Along one wall of the lounge is a display of traditional musical instruments, and some evenings they have musicians playing in the restaurant. In many ways it was just like a top class hotel in any country. It was strange to sit and listen to Mozart one minute and walk out into the streets of Lahore the next. At about 10.30 pm on our last night in Pakistan a raucous band started up somewhere in the street behind our hotel. It had a thumping bass drum and loud, out of tune, trombones, trumpets and clarinets. Amazingly, they were playing a tune in triple time.

Egypt

Egypt is often seen as the political, social and cultural leader of the Muslim world. Central to its policies are those to do with education, which is considered the life-blood of the state. For historical reasons, Western influences dominate the education system in Egypt today. With the renewed calls for Islamisation in all aspects of society, education is necessarily in the forefront. A survey carried out in 1998 found that amongst a literate student population a large majority considered the national system of education as too 'Westernised': most respondents were in favour of imposing a religious education requirement where none exists at present. And a majority affirmed that a university with a more Islamic orientation would enhance the quality of education (Cook, 1999b). This has caused a dilemma for politicians: on the one hand they realise that the majority of people in the country would like a return to stronger Islamic traditions, believing that Western style education is 'doing immeasurable damage to the moral, spiritual and ethical values of Islamic culture and heritage' (Cook, 2000, p478). On the other hand they are anxious not to be seen to be promoting or condoning Islamic extremism.

Most of the Egyptians who influence the curriculum in schools are acknowledged to be liberal, or secular, Muslims who do not support the more traditional Islamic outlook.

As Cook (2000, p488) put it:

> Secularists represent a marginal percentage of the total of the Egyptian population but exert a disproportionate influence on educational policy.

Accordingly, the officials I talked to espoused music in schools. But this did not mean it was easy to get permission to look at the music lessons, and it took me ten days of visiting various government offices in Cairo before this was eventually given. Apparently the hold up came from the need to ensure that I was not on any international terrorist list. The authorisation I eventually received permitted me to go to any school within a specified time frame. I have used material from the visits to schools which were willing to allow me access and were happy to be recorded.

During the many hours that I sat around in offices, most of the administrators were happy to talk to me. Some spoke English, in which case I had direct information, but others I could only communicate with through my interpreter. At the Department for Education I was sent to the office of the Head of Music for Schools. His deputy told me that in Egypt all children did music, whatever their religion, and there were no problems. However, he did understand the difficulty because he had taught music in Kuwait where there were many people who objected to it on religious grounds. He also said that before Mullahs are allowed to do the *adhan* (the call to prayer), they have singing lessons to improve their voices.

During the first part of my time in Egypt I stayed with a Muslim family in Cairo. I also spent some time with another Muslim family who had two children at secondary school. The daughter told me that music is compulsory until the age of 14, when there is a choice between art and music and sometimes computers. At her school there is only a choice between art and music, 80 per cent choosing the latter. It is almost unheard of for a pupil to opt out, although occasionally a girl will say that she is not allowed to sing. She told me that although they all know that music is not allowed in Islam it doesn't make any difference to their lifestyle. The son said that although music is compulsory in his school, the boys do not take it seriously because they are not tested in it. Out of about 75 boys in the year only four or five choose to continue with music post 14. These families provided me with a better understanding of the culture.

Children in Egypt are tested in order to establish which school they will go to. These tests begin at the age of 4 and continue right through their education. To gain a place at the top schools the pupils need to achieve 95per cent in their tests. All parents who can afford it have private tutors for their children as well. This continues right through their education, even if they are at the top schools, because the teaching in state education alone is not sufficient for them to

A music room in a secondary school in Cairo

stay in the top 5 per cent. The schools I saw were in the top sector and, in Egyptian terms, well provided with equipment including some instruments. Hanging around the walls of the music room at the preparatory school were many percussion instruments and a few string instruments, but the class only ever did singing. There were 40 girls, about half wearing headscarves, and most of whom appeared to be singing. The songs were religious or nationalistic; pop songs were not allowed even though most of the girls listened to these at home. The class singing was poor, with no attention to pitch. One girl wanted to be a professional singer. She had private lessons and sang very well. Although this school is better equipped than schools with less able pupils, they could not afford a keyboard and went to the senior school to use one. The music teacher found his job dull and needed to tutor in the evenings as well in order to earn enough to keep his family.

In the secondary school music is optional after the age of 14. This school also has only the top 5 per cent of girls, of whom about 60 per cent choose music. Girls rarely object to music on religious grounds, although occasionally one will refuse to sing. In the classroom there is a drum kit, played by a male teacher. The lessons consist of theory, history and practical, much of which is the singing of patriotic songs. Some girls played guitar, mandolin or keyboard, and the rest sang. There was a music curriculum and the teacher has lesson plans for all lessons. These plans are similar to those you might find in any UK school and include examples of Western music.

I had difficulty gaining entry to the Academy of Arts High Institute for Arab Music in Cairo and eventually gained admittance only because my interpreter had a nephew who could sign me in. Even so, I had to leave my passport with security at the entrance. Instrumental music and singing was coming from all corners of the building, and the pressure on space for practising was as intense as in any London music college. At the Academy I interviewed a lecturer who had been teaching there for 16 years. The lecturer told me that during his career he had visited Pakistan, where he had come across several instances of people refusing to do music. He said that in Cairo he thought only about 1 per cent refused. He said that although in the past there had been problems with girls being allowed to perform, now it was perfectly acceptable. However, circumstances surrounding this visit did not bear out the idea that music was fine. When we were sitting in the grounds of the music college waiting to see the lecturer my interpreter said:

> Look at all these girls; you can see they are no good. Look at the way they are dressed.

Although some were dressed in western clothes there were only one or two who I would have considered to be wearing seductive clothing, yet he condemned them all and said he would not let his daughter attend this college. This comment appeared strange bearing in mind that he had said music was acceptable and had suggested taking me to see belly dancing. There were several armed guards at the entrances to the building. All men in Egypt do National Service and it is common to see two or three armed soldiers stationed at the corners of streets, but far more were in evidence at the music college. The reason given for this was that if Islamic fundamentalists were to attack anywhere then it would be likely to be a music establishment because of music being considered *haram* in Islam.

Although music is on the curriculum for all government schools in Egypt it is clearly controversial. Despite my letter of authority, two schools were not prepared to admit me. At the first, an elementary

Nehad and Sebai, students from the High Institute for Arab Music, performing for me in a coffee house in Cairo.

school in a poor area in Cairo, a board with a music stave and birds singing hung behind the head's desk. This seemed to bode well, but the head rejected my pass, saying that I needed to have a specific authority for his school rather than general permission for any schools in order to see any classes. I asked whether I could talk to the music teacher. She was sent for. By this time there were nine people in the office waiting to see what would happen. They were all pouring over my permission letter and finally decided that they had to ring a higher authority. Eventually it was decided that I could not talk to the music teacher either. I asked if I could take a photo of the picture behind his desk and this was also refused. I wanted to know why he was so concerned about my seeing classes and talking to the music teacher. He said he was afraid of the use I would make of the information. He thought it might not be good for Egypt and might get him into trouble.

The next school I tried, again in a poor area and for lower ability children, also refused me entrance, saying that they did not do music. On being pressed they said that they did some theory but had no instruments and did no singing either. Music, they said, was a low priority subject and lessons were often cancelled in order to do something else and there were none that day, or the next...! My guide told me the lower sector had very limited resources and may well not do any music even though it is supposed to be compulsory.

I had hoped to visit al Azhar University, one of the foremost Islamic universities in the world, but my request was turned down by letter before I arrived in Cairo. I did however manage to interview Abdel Mobdy Ahmed, a retired *Sheihk* from al Azhar, at his home. He did not speak English but his daughter Hala translated for me. He was educated at al Azhar University, where the curriculum was totally dedicated to Islamic Studies. He went on to postgraduate studies and obtained a teaching certificate. He was then appointed a *Sheihk* at al Azhar where his duties were to revise all books before they were published. Every book on Islam from anywhere in the world during that period had to go to al Azhar before it could be published. After this he was sent as a preacher to Algeria, Indonesia, Lebanon, Syria, UAE, Thailand and Singapore. He went to Algeria at the time of its independence from France in order to 'make it Arabic again'.

I was surprised to learn that music had been taught as a subject at al Azhar until 1956. I asked him why it was taken off the curriculum:

AA: It was then stopped because of the reform to the educational system at al Azhar. They removed what they thought of as extras – music and sport – because the al Azhar educational system was overloaded. They now study the universal topics like mathematics, sciences, languages and religious education. So it may be there just wasn't time to do music as well.

DH: I have heard that in some places the *muezzin* have singing lessons before they do the *adhan*. Is this still the case at al Azhar?

AA: No, if this happens it would be a private arrangement. It is not taught as part of the curriculum at al Azhar.

I asked Ahmed whether he agreed that music was not prohibited in the Qur'an.

AA: Yes, those who say that music is haram have no evidence to support those views.

DH: If we move on to the *ahadith*: my understanding is that there are weak and strong *hadith* so could you tell me which are the *hadith* that we should accept?

64

AA: In the *hadith* of Bukhari, this is one of the strong *ahadith*: he tells us to entertain hearts, one hour yes and one hour no, to maintain a balance. Interesting hearts one yes and one hour no, because hearts get bored and sick, and if they get bored and sick they are blind.

Since Shar'ia Law denies any value to a musician's testimony, I was interested in how he thought musicians were viewed in society, given that he found music acceptable. He disagrees with that interpretation of the Shar'ia Law:

AA: This is a false belief. I studied this under my professor who was one of the most important professors in al Azhar and who was considered a pioneer of cultural activity.

His view is that a musician is as worthwhile as any other human being and should be treated as such. I asked about whether it was as acceptable for women to perform as men and whether musical instruments were allowed.

AA: It's not widely acceptable for women to perform but it's not *haram*, it's more *mubah*.

DH: Is that in terms of singing at all or just performing in front of men?

AA: Not in front of men.

DH: Do you see any problem with children post puberty doing music lessons together?

AA: It's preferable to be separated at this stage.

DH: What about the situation with musical instruments? Are there some that are not allowed or has this also come about through tradition?

AA: It's cultural or personal preference, it's not to do with religion.

We talked about changing the language we use when talking about music to promote a better understanding of the meaning of music in a western context.

DH: Some people have felt that it would be better not to use the term music because it is associated with secular activities. It has been suggested by the al Faruqis in America that the term 'sound arts' would be better. What do you think?

AA: Changing names or terms would not shift something from being a sin or not. I think some of the people who regard music as a sin have read a history of Muhammad that said that he used to isolate himself from musical parties where they had dancers who used to move and wear extremely liberal clothes, which went against his morality. Probably those who think of music as a sin are thinking of this when they say that music is *haram*. Some people during the time of Muhammad used to hold parties especially for young people in order to distract them from the words of the Prophet.

We went on to talk about Sufism.

DH: Can we talk for a moment about the Sufi tradition. It is said that when Sufis go into a trance bad thoughts could enter their minds, or that because their passions are involved it could be dangerous. What is your view?

AA: Muslims should not base their traditions or ideas on Sufis because sometimes they have extremist ideas which can be in conflict with each other. I don't support the Sufi tradition.

I was particularly interested to find out what a *Sheihk* from al-Azhar would feel about singing and dancing within the confines of a mosque.

DH: Why do you think Sufi dancing is allowed in the citadel for visitors to go and see?

AA: This is just for tourists, for show, it is not for Muslims.

DH: I am surprised therefore that it is allowed in the citadel because I would have thought it would have been somewhere that did not have religious significance.

AA: The citadel is an area, it is not the centre of Islam; many people refuse to go and pray over there. Mohammad Mosque is not such a valuable mosque for Muslim belief or faith.

DH: Could you explain that to me a bit more? It's very interesting.

AA: The Sufi tradition of ceremonies and of dancing until you lose consciousness goes against all that Mohammad said. Mohammad said, be moderate when you pray to God; you don't need to shout or raise your voice.

Turkey

My contact in Turkey was Dr Recep Kaymakcan, a lecturer at Sakarya University who also teaches religious instruction at a private school attached to the university. Turkey is a secular country and no signs of religion are allowed in public life. Women in government offices are not allowed to wear the hijab and girls in school cannot cover their heads either. Few concessions are made for people to attend Friday prayers and Islam cannot be taught in schools, other than as part of a general religious and moral education course. State schools, and most independent schools, are all co-ed, which many Muslims find difficult to accept. In the elections of 2002 the populace removed the long standing secular party and brought in the *Adalet ve Kalkinma Partisi* (Justice and Development Party or JDP), which is Islamist in its roots, to power. The new government is powerless to change Turkey's secular state because it is enshrined in the constitution. However, the Islamists have continued to perceive secularisation as an attempt to transplant Western laws, mores, and institutions on Turkey, therefore displacing the traditional Islamic values. The debate between Islamists and secularists continues. This conversation is heightened by the renewed call for Muslims to go back to their traditional values, on the one hand, and on the other for Turkey to become more like Western governments in order to enhance their chances of full membership of the European Community.

Kaymakcan told me that the 80,000 imams in the country are appointed and paid for by the government, which shows the determination of Turkey to remain a secular constitution. It is also illegal for imams to express any views about education. There may be some who express views privately about music being taught in schools, but they cannot say anything publicly. Against this it can be seen that many of the people are still affirming their Islamic foundations. In the population as a whole between 40 and 50 per cent of men observe Friday prayers. Women rarely go to the mosque but are allowed to pray at the back if they wish. Two thirds of the country fast during Ramadan, when men and women often go to the mosque together, although they still pray in separate areas. There are no regular madrassas, but 1,000,000 children go to summer schools to learn the Qur'an. There are also *Imam-Hatip* (prayer-leader/ preacher) schools that are growing in popularity. The main objective of these schools was to train the clergy to carry out religious services, but they have become transformed into more mainstream schools to cater for the children of conservative and religious parents. Pak (2004, p337), wrote:

> If we consider that people are socialised according to a culturally determined orientation and that schools play a significant role in constructing social reality then one can expect schools to play a major part in determining the outcome of the ongoing 'cultural war' in Turkey.

Ali Perret, Professor of Music at Bilgi University in Istanbul, gave me some background on the musical tradition of Turkey:

AP: In Turkey music is important and there are different styles of music. There is music that came from the palaces – more elite type of music, music for the Ottomans – and there's folk music which is rich in every region of Turkey. It is still played a lot and is danced to a lot and is very colourful and different in each area. That's still going on. And then there's the Mehlavi tradition. It's not like the Shi'ites in Iran, it's different. It goes back to the Shaman thinking and it's very typical of the music in Anatolia. It's like 20% of the population in Turkey and they have their own music. It's not really religious but there is mystical thinking to it.

DH: Not like Sufi music?

AP: No, Sufi music is more religious, meditation music.

DH: And where do women musicians fit into the musical tradition?

AP: There are a lot. If you go to the Conservatories, the Turkish classical ones rather than the Western ones, there is not any problem for women. In Turkish music education there are now more women than there were and you see more, sometimes all female bands in hotels and concerts and things like that. Even now there's a new thing that I read in the newspaper that in Sufi music, the religious music, they didn't have any women but now the dancers and musicians are sometimes women. That is new. That was the last thing that we expected women to get into but it's happening here. There has always been music amongst women, in the harem and so on, but not mixed before. And there's one professor who's written a book and done concerts of 18th and 19th century female Turkish composers. So there's quite a tradition with women in Turkish classical music

DH: Most music in Turkey is monophonic. Is this a cultural or religious custom?

AP: In Turkey, as with many other countries, that is true, the music is monophonic. The words are on their own or, if accompanied by instruments they play the same thing. But inside the melodic structure there is harmony sometimes. They simply use the 5th and the 4th and sometimes the 2nd even within solo playing. Probably the only thing that doesn't have harmonies is the traditional folk music and some classical Turkish music. The rhythm always goes with the words which is why we often have some strange metres.

DH: But I haven't seen Turkish classical music taught in schools. Is there a music curriculum in Turkey?

AP: In normal schools, primary schools, there are two classes you can pick up, either art or music, you can't have both...

DH: ...and what age is that?

AP: Starting at 7. It used to be 5 but now it is 7 years, but the music education is not any good and the teachers are not any good either.

DH: I haven't seen any listening or appraising or composition.

AP: They used to but that changed when I was a student. Now they play the mandolin or flute (your recorder) or harmonium, but after the 80s it changed a bit and I think mostly what they do now is theory, recorders and singing. Up until the 80s there were something like 110 choirs singing and the music was simple folk music, and they sang in two parts.

Schools in Turkey consist of kindergarten beginning from aged 3, 4 or 5 to aged 7; primary, aged 7 to 15 and high, aged 16 to 18, although some pupils do a fourth year at high school if they do a preparatory year with extended English. I found that music is taught to most children from aged 7 to 14, the exception being in some primary schools where there is a choice between music and art. All pupils are expected to sing and many play recorders, although these have to be provided by the pupils and not all children have them. Without question these lessons are enjoyed. Although the general level of music education in schools is poor, Turkey does provide specialist music schools for talented pupils. The conservatory system starts at the age of 8 and is a twelve-year programme. There are between six and ten conservatories in various cities and they are free. Children come from all over Turkey and live at the conservatories. As well as this there are music high schools, both state and private, in about five large cities.

The first school I visited was in Sakarya. My introduction to this area of Turkey, which is 120 kilometers east of Istanbul, was from my host at the pension I was staying at in Istanbul. There was great hilarity because of the many misunderstandings in our communication. It was some time before I worked out that Sakarya was the part of Turkey devastated by earthquakes in 1999. My host constantly seemed to refer to it being the 'oatcake' centre due to the difficulty the Turkish have with the English sounds 'th' and 'qu'. Visiting the town of Adapazari three and a half years after the earthquake, it was

Children in a dance class in Adapazari, Turkey

apparent that much of the city had been reduced to rubble. This was one of the reasons why they no longer have many foreign visitors and I was made to feel very welcome.

Loud music heralded the change in lessons at all the schools I visited but the first lesson I attended, a folk dancing lesson, had no accompaniment. The teacher had a good voice and sang much of the time but had not considered using a cassette recorder to play a tape. The children were aged seven and clearly enjoyed the lesson. They happily danced together boy/girl/boy/girl and sometimes sang as well, but seemed to have little idea about pitch. The children in this private school do dance until the age of 15 and all lessons are mixed sex, which is very unusual for Muslims in other countries.

My second lesson was with a form teacher who also has an orchestra. This consists of un-tuned percussion instruments which they sing along to. The children sang and danced while they played, but with little sense of either rhythm or pitch. They were, however, very confident. At the end of one song they came to the front individually, danced, bowed and returned to the rest of the group. Only one child did not perform but he too came to the front and bowed before going straight back. Having percussion instruments in school was a rarity, limited to affluent schools. None of the schools I visited has a music room or a piano but this private school has plans for both.

The majority of my time in Adapazari was spent with the music teacher in a private school where most of the lessons followed the same pattern. He would begin with breathing exercises, then they sang a scale, which he accompanied on his mandolin. After singing a few songs, either folk or nationalistic, those in the class who had recorders would play them. The government dictates which books schools can use and many of the songs came from one of the set books. The book in use in this school is *Flkogretin Muzik 8* (Saydam, 2000). Although there are several levels of this book in this school the same one was used for all classes aged 7 to 15. There appeared to be no difference in the content of the lessons whatever year group was being taught. The book consists of some music theory and history as well as songs.

A lesson taught to 8 to 9 year olds was typical of the plan of each lesson. It began with breathing exercises and then they sang a scale with the mandolin. The pitching was very poor, but the tessitura was too high for most of the pupils. One girl then did some conducting while the teacher played the violin because a string had broken on his mandolin. It was often difficult to understand exactly what was happening because the teacher did not speak English. He continued to play the violin while children drew on the board. One drew a picture of a boy with a hoop around him, another a small plant growing into a tree and then a forest, and a third a sheep. Presumably they were representing the music. Only five children in that class had recorders. They were also taught about rhythm with a semibreve, minim, crotchet and pair of quavers being drawn on the board.

Another interesting class was of 14 to 15 year olds. They were very noisy although again they sang enthusiastically. In the lesson I saw they were learning a new song which they did by first writing down the words and then learning the tune from the violin. The motivation in the classes was mostly good but if children did not want to take part they seemed to be allowed to do other things; some of the children were even doing work for a different subject. This class was particularly unruly and the teacher just concentrated on those who wanted to learn. They also used *Muzik 8* by Refik Saydam. This series of books has songs from around the world, pages about rhythm, some information about Mozart, Beethoven and Schubert and a section about how a scale is made up. As well as major and minor (harmonic and melodic), there is also dogal, which is the aeolian mode, commonly used in Turkey. There is nothing about harmony in the book and composition is not taught either.

A music lesson in an independent school in Adapazari, Turkey

The question of pitch was extremely interesting: all music, to be either sung or played on the recorder, is learnt by tonic sol-fa, and the pupils appear to understand it. However, the notes sung bear no relation to the pitch, the pupils intoning on a monotone, doh and soh for example sounding exactly the same. The teacher, a good musician himself, did nothing to correct pitch at any time during lessons, so many of the songs were tuneless. This was despite the fact that they were practising for a performance the following week. Because there were not enough music lessons to fill the whole time-table I also became an English assistant in English classes. The classes always wanted to hear me sing English songs, and I taught them some as well. Although I would not have attempted to correct their pitch in music lessons I felt that I could in these lessons. In nearly every case the pupils were able to pitch accurately but it is obviously not thought to be important and they certainly enjoy their singing very much. I did have the chance during my stay in Turkey to listen and talk to some fine musicians, including the music teacher in this school, and for them rhythm and pitch were important. An occurrence in the staff room at the independent school in Adapazari indicated the love of music in Turkey. One afternoon break the music teacher played his *balimah* (a larger version of an *oud*) in the staff-room and the rest of the teachers all sang to me. I cannot imagine this happening in a school in England.

All the schools I visited also had a school marching band, which appears to be a standard feature. The bands consist of cymbals, drums and bugles, and band practice was held during the lunch break. One band I watched for half an hour did not move anywhere. Occasionally they marched on the spot but more often they just played the same rhythm over and over again. The bugles rarely played, and then only one note. In one band I watched, the players kept their bugles under their arms and did not play them at all because they did not know how to.

The ratio of children in state to private education is 3:1. Most state schools have a different intake in the morning and afternoon and have only six lessons a day. This means that subjects such as music, art and folk dancing are often limited. The classes in the state school in Sakarya that I visited have between 30 and 60 pupils. They mostly sing and play the recorder, if they have one. Again there is little attention to pitch. The school starts at 7.50am and finishes at 6.00pm with two shifts of children. The teachers each have to teach six lessons a day and they have a break of ten minutes between each lesson. Apparently none of the children in the state school has private instrumental lessons. As well as the marching band there is a choir at weekends, attended by 50 boys and girls between the ages of 12 and 15. In lessons they sometimes listen to western classical music, Beethoven and Mozart, which the children enjoy. Some of the music lessons in the state school were very good. The teacher had a good voice and harmonised their singing. In one particular class of 22 boys and 14 girls (aged 12), the singing was excellent and several boys wanted to sing on their own. The behaviour in the class was not particularly good but all except six pupils were singing enthusiastically. This music teacher seemed to have a much more organised approach to his teaching. All the pupils have to do a music exam at the end of each year at which they are tested on their recorder playing. There are no public exams.

In Istanbul the school I visited was in Kestepe, a poor area where many immigrants and gypsies live. School is compulsory from 7.30-12.45 and then there are optional extra lessons in English, Turkish, maths and science until 4.30. The classes are generally of 34 to 36, and again the lessons consist of singing and recorders.

Boys in a music class in Istanbul

The classes were generally well behaved and girls and boys often shared desks. As with the schools in Adapazari, solfa was taught but the pitch was poor. Typically about eighteen children had recorders and while they learnt to play them the others sat and did nothing. The theory part of the lesson consisted of learning how to construct the major, minor and dorian mode scales.

Bilgi University is in Kestepe and it carries out an interesting programme of music education for children, set up because the standard of school music in the surrounding area is so low. Haluk Polat, a lecturer at the university, gave me this example of the standard of musical knowledge:

> I asked them (the children), to find out the name of an Indian percussion instrument. They asked their music teacher, I guess, and they gave me the answer of Ghandi!

The university selected 60 pupils, aged 11 to 18, who are given lessons in basic ear training, listening and history. They also sing in a choir. The emphasis is on the Western classical tradition but occasionally they include some Turkish popular or art music. In their 2nd year the students have the opportunity to learn a musical instrument. Music in schools is almost entirely monophonic but this university choir

Students in the music evening class programme at Bilgi University, Istanbul

sings in parts, either a capella or accompanied by piano. The class I attended consisted of seven boys and thirteen girls. They started by singing *California Dreaming*, very nicely in harmony, then went on to learning a new Turkish song. They also did music appreciation in which they learnt about Aretha Franklin and the blues. In an interview with Haluk Polat I discovered that as well as this they did music analysis of western music, beginning with Gregorian Chant. When I was there they had reached the Renaissance and were going to go on to Baroque. Another part of their course is basic ear training. Composition is not included in their classes but Polat did not see any reason why they might not do it in the future. The project was only in its second year of a six year programme and they hope to include many more opportunities for the students.

Part of my interview with Polat consisted of questions to do with musical instruments, harmony, and boys and girls singing together.

DH: In England there are three main areas that are contentious for some Muslims: the use of harmony or musical instruments because they detract from the words, and the issue of boys and girls singing together at secondary school. What is the situation here?

HP: Turkey is very different from the other Muslim countries. But
        they are only accustomed to sing in monophony, they are not
        used to harmony or polyphony, this is the main problem on the
        musical side. But on the social side in Istanbul, and in this part
        in particular, there will be no problem with boys and girls sing-
        ing together, but in some parts of Anatolia, and some high
        schools, boys and girls would not be together like this. Our pro-
        gramme here is different; this is not an obligation, they choose
        it.

DH: So in school they have to be together but out of school they
        may choose not to be?

HP: Yes

Malaysia

In Ramona Tahir's doctoral thesis (1996), she asked, 'How may
Islamic principles be implemented in the Malaysian music curriculum?' She recorded the views of two teachers, the dean of a school,
a headmaster and a managing director. The first teacher she spoke
to suggested that they should sing songs with the theme of God and
aspects of humanity; that they should co-operate with those who
know about music in Islam; and they should expose non-Muslim
music teachers to the issues of Islam in order to be able to implement them. The second teacher refused to answer the questions because he was afraid to release statements concerning Islamic laws.
The dean said that what is taught in music classes, as well as how it
is taught, must abide by Islamic values and principles. The managing director made four suggestions, namely: a committee committed to both Islam and music needs to be selected for the task of
investigating the issue of music in Islam and implementing a school
music curriculum consistent with Islam; the formation of guidelines
based on the Shar'iah Law is necessary; the establishment of a re-
source and reference centre for the study and development of music
acceptable in Islam; and through the existence of a system which is
Islamic politically, economically and socially. The headmaster did
not think it possible to resolve the controversy regarding music
education and Islam.

Four conclusions can be drawn from Tahir's thesis: music education
is permissible in Malaysia provided it occurs in context and under
conditions sanctioned by Islam; there is a need for an alternative
term for music because it has negative connotations in the Islamic
world; music education in Malaysia should promote music which is

approved by Islam; and all concerned with music education in Malaysia need to be united and focused in their mission if a music education which is consistent with Islam is to exist in Malaysia. Note that in Tahir's work music only refers to singing because the issues surrounding musical instruments are far more complicated and contentious.

Non-Muslim countries

This section looks at Finland, USA and Canada – Western countries that, in common with the UK, have a large Muslim population. The information on Finland comes from an unpublished MA thesis specifically about Helsinki, whilst the USA school I have reported on may or may not be typical. The material from Canada is based on research carried out by a student studying for a Masters Degree and again refers to a specific school.

Finland

Muslims from Somalia have settled in Helsinki. In the conclusion to their unpublished master's thesis, Klemetti and Ritvaniemi (1998) made several points that confirmed much of my research with Muslims in the UK. In Somalia the word 'music' is used differently: singing is not considered to be music or music making; music only refers to instrumental music. Singing is very important in the Somali tradition with families taking part in a variety of songs from nursery rhymes to complicated arrangements with vocal accompaniments, but they don't play tuned instruments. Music is not seen as having any point in itself; it is always serving some other purpose and the words are functional. Because the Somalis believe it is *haram,* there is no instrumental music in Somali schools, and although there is singing in some lessons they don't have specific lessons for singing. The parents questioned were critical of music lessons in primary and secondary schools in Helsinki and over half of those interviewed said they did not want their children to take part in music lessons at school. However, they were not unhappy about there being some musical component in other lessons. Some parents had told their children not to take part in music lessons and on the whole the headteachers had agreed to this, but only one parent knew what actually happened in music lessons.

America

My contact in America is the Dean of Students of one of the largest Islamic schools in America. Aisha Ahmed is a Muslim and has two sons who go to a state school because she and her husband want them to have a well-rounded education and be able to participate in the arts. All the staff at the Islamic school are Muslim, mostly originating from the Middle East, but they have been educated in the USA. There are also some American or European born teachers who have converted to Islam. There is no tradition of music in the school. It caters for various degrees of Islamic strictness and the imam at the local mosque has a say in what is acceptable. Music is not offered as a subject but the pre-school and kindergarten classes do sing learning songs. Aisha has always held that music is very important and has tried to establish music in the school. She said:

> When I began teaching here I suggested that there should be a keyboard accompaniment to the songs. Our students have great difficulty singing in unison and in tune, and their musical skills are, on the whole, undeveloped. While younger members of the staff, including the principal, liked the idea and encouraged me to present the idea to the board, it was not approved. There was a fear that members of the audience would walk out, especially if the imam did.

Instead she decided to compose some simple songs and teach them to the children herself. She became known as the 'Song Lady' and became the most popular teacher in the elementary school. She said: 'The students had been starved of any musical experience and they looked forward to my visits to the classroom'. She then introduced a morning assembly and each class was given a week once every quarter when they gave a short presentation, including some singing, to the rest of the school. Because Aisha had musical knowledge and experience she helped the class teachers who had no musical background. These assemblies have become an important part of the life of the school, but only at elementary level.

Some of the governors are beginning to come around to the idea of music and one of the founders of the school has said that he sees no harm in music, and maybe in the future the pupils might have a band. Aisha does not envisage this being generally acceptable for some time but thinks she may be able to introduce some un-tuned percussion as an extra curricular activity. She wrote:

> Naturally as a music educator and someone who believes in the teachings of Islam, and converted of my own free will, I feel that the

children are somewhat deprived. As the chief disciplinarian in the school, I feel that many of our problems would be solved if our students were able to have a variety of artistic outlets. To this end, I have convinced the faculty that we need to arrange extra curricular activities of an artistic nature during the coming year. I myself plan to start some kind of choral activity. The older girls will be able to perform to each other at female functions. I have also suggested an art club, to provide formal art lessons, and a drama club was even mentioned (separate sexes of course).

Canada

Sally Ann Martin, from the University of Toronto, carried out her MA research during 2003-4 in an elementary public school and a kindergarten where she had taught for five years. The school populations consisted of over 90 per cent Muslims from Pakistan, India and Afghanistan and few children in the kindergarten spoke English. Her research was divided into two sections: the first looked specifically into the kinds of music that Grade 5 (age 9-10), mostly Muslim, girls liked. The other part of her research was based on her experience teaching these girls.

The first part of the study consisted of a listening component and a short questionnaire about popular music videos. The listening consisted of ten excerpts of school music, holiday concert repertoire, well-known classical orchestral and choral repertoire, and recent pop music. The music almost unanimously favoured was recent pop music, but a piece that the choir had performed was also appreciated highly. In response to the questions about music videos, the majority of students said that they did watch them with their parents, although one student said that her mother often turned them off. Several students said that parts of the videos made them feel uncomfortable, in which case they either ignored them or turned them off. When asked why the pupils watched the music videos the response was always 'due to peer pressure'.

In her experience of teaching children aged 3 to 9, Martin found few problems arose regarding the participation of the Muslim children in music classes. She was aware, however, that after the age of 11 significant issues became apparent. The main difficulty arose when the choirs participated in the Kiwanis Music Festival, where the performance venue was a Christian church. A letter was sent to the parents outlining the nature of the festival, saying that it was a school trip that was part of their music education and not part of any religious worship. The first year many Muslim parents refused permission, and none of the parents accepted the invitation to accompany the visit, or the chance to speak to Martin about it. The Muslim parents who allowed their children to attend told her that there was nothing in the Qur'an to prevent their children entering a Christian building. However, as years have gone by more parents, aunts and uncles have begun to accompany the visit and even to film their children taking part.

5

A case study of a Pakistani family in Pakistan and England

This chapter tells the story of a family who are split between Pakistan and England. Although it deals with music it also gives an insight into the lives of this family. I believe it is important to look beyond the immediate issue to acquire deeper understanding of the culture. This chapter is based on notes from the journal I kept while staying with the family in Pakistan. But these notes cannot stand alone so I have added comments made on my return to England. In order to make sense of these strands in the context of this book I have provided another strand to link them with other aspects of music from my research. Because I would like readers to be able to read this chapter like a diary I used different fonts to highlight each strand: extracts from my journal are in this font with comments in *italics*, and normal print for thoughts linking the case study to aspects of music. Given the complicated structure of the family, I have introduced each member and included a family tree.

The family living in Pakistan

Muhammad is married to *Jumila* and they live on the ground floor of their home in a town I will call Arun in North Western Pakistan, with Jumila's mother who is 90. Muhammad and Jumila had three sons and five daughters. The eldest son, also called Muhammad, married Zainab, but died 10 years ago. After Muhammad there followed five daughters: Leila, Sunita, Mehnaz, Shazeen and Fatima and then two more sons, Ahsan and Waqas. In our story we do not

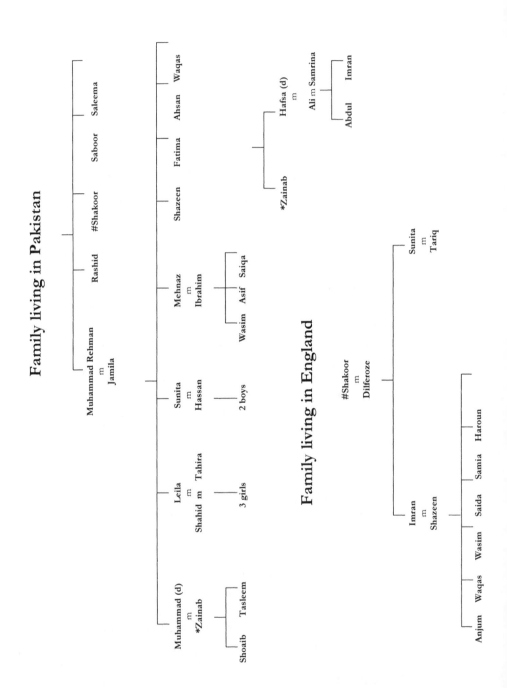

Family living in Pakistan

Family living in England

meet the two youngest sisters or the two youngest brothers, none of whom live in Arun.

Zainab and her children Shoaib, aged 23, and Tasleem, aged 18, live on the top floor of Muhammad and Jumila's house. Zainab qualified as a teacher before she met her husband Muhammad. She spent the first ten years of her married life in Iran, where Muhammad was a doctor. They came back to Pakistan when her children were 8 and 3 because they felt the children would have a better education in Pakistan. Zainab and Muhammad moved in with Muhammad (senior) and Jumila (her in-laws), but did not find it easy to adjust to living with them. Zainab felt that as the eldest son, Muhammad was expected to do too much for the family. She wanted to run her own household as she had in Iran. Muhammad died the same year as Zainab's sister, Hafsa, and soon after her mother. This was a difficult time for Zainab and she was pleased that she had her teaching job to go to, which she had re-started when Tasleem was 4. Zainab teaches in an independent school belonging to the Beaconhouse group.

Shoaib is Zainab's son. He is 23 and in his final year at medical college. Shoaib has taken responsiblity for his mother and sister, Tasleem, because his father is dead, even though their grandfather is still alive. He is expected to do all the family shopping as well as sort out a complicated family financial situation, while maintaining a social life and revising for his exams.

Tasleem is Zainab's daughter and Shoaib's sister. She is 18 and has just finished school. She has done well in her exams and is about to apply to universities. She is intelligent and outgoing but does not leave the house on her own except to visit a close friend who lives nearby.

Leila is an education officer in charge of girls' schools in a large part of the country outside Arun. Although married, she no longer lives with her husband.

Sunita works in a girls' high school situated in the bazaar area. She speaks no English. She is married to Hassan and has two sons.

Mehnaz and *Ibrahim* and their three children *Wasim*, 17, *Asif*, 15 and *Saiqa*, 11 lived in England for seven years. Ibrahim is a banker. They would like to live in England again. All speak excellent English.

Ali is Zainab's brother-in-law. His first wife, Zainab's sister, died about 10 years ago. He then married *Samrina*. They have two sons, Abdul and Imran. Ali is a banker and Samrina teaches Pakistani Studies in a college for students aged 16 to 18. Zainab is closer to Ali and Samrina than to her husband's relatives.

The family living in England

Shakoor moved to England just over 30 years ago, followed shortly after by his wife *Fatima*. They already had a son, Imran, born in Pakistan, and their daughter, Sunita was born in England 29 years ago.

Shazeen came to England to marry *Imran* 20 years ago. They now have six children Anjum, Waqas, Wasim, Saida, Samia and Haroun, aged between 18 years and 18 months.

Sunita is a religious education teacher at a Sixth Form college. She married *Tariq* in Pakistan in the summer of 1998 and he moved to England in 1999. He is a qualified geography teacher but his qualification is not recognised in England.

Extracts from my journal and commentary

19 October *The Khans live in a large house. Muhammad and Jumila, grandparents to Shoaib and Tasleem, live downstairs with Jumila's mother. At 90 she still squats on the floor in a way that I would find agonising; I suppose she has done it all her life. Outside is a yard with a shed where their servant lives with her husband and two children. Zainab, Shoaib and Tasleem live upstairs. They have two large bedrooms with washing facilities attached, a big living room and a small kitchen. They share the servant with the grandparents. Rachel and I were given the bedroom usually shared by Zainab and Tasleem because it has a European style toilet. It has a double bed which Zainab and Tasleem have shared for many years. Zainab and Tasleem have moved to Shoaib's room and he is staying downstairs with his grandparents.*

Tasleem had made lunch for us which we had at 3pm when Zainab returned from school. She seems to think we will not want to eat Pakistani food and has cooked Chinese. Our reception has been wonderful; they are delighted to see us and everything is relaxed and friendly right from the start.

The noise in the evening was amazing. I asked Tasleem where the birds were. They were making an incredible noise and sounded like an aviary. She looked bemused and said, 'In the trees'. In addition there was the call to prayer from two different mosques, sounding as if they were competing with their different tunes. We could also hear the musicians from the nearby military academy practising. I couldn't work out the instruments because they were not distinct enough but it didn't sound like a western band.

Many Muslims have difficulty understanding that to western ears their *adhan* – call to prayer – sounds like music. Much of this is to do with their term for 'music', which tends to denote secular music. This difficulty with terminology causes problems. Mosques within the same area do not actually compete with each other, but much attention is paid to the 'musical' quality of the voices of the mullahs who perform the *adhan*. This was the only place in Pakistan where we heard band music playing – a legacy from the days of Imperial rule. The army is clearly still run along British lines. I was surprised at how much importance is still given to British institutions. The fee-paying schools all teach in English even though Urdu is the official language. Although Pakistan is trying to establish its own identity, this is about being a separate state from India; it does not seek to outlaw British standards.

20 October Today I am at Zainab's school. It is a Beaconhouse school which opened on 2 March 1991, but the first Beaconhouse in Pakistan is now 25 years old. It teaches all subjects in English, except Islamia and Urdu, and sets out to model English schools as far as possible, even following some of the National Curriculum. It is a fee-paying school for 4-15 yr olds. *Due to parental pressure years 6 and 7 are taught in separate sex classes. The parents would like this extended throughout the upper school but it is financially unviable.* Assembly was very military. The classes marched on to what looked like a parade ground to the beat of a drum. All the children stood to attention while a junior class took assembly. A boy recited a section of the Qur'an from memory and then about eight children gave a talk about traffic signs! During the chanting from the Qur'an the whole school folded their arms. Then they sang the National Anthem, again standing to attention. Do children at school in England even know the National Anthem? At the end the head asked if anyone had noticed anything wrong with the recitation. Several people had and the boy then did it again in order to be corrected. At the end there was more music and a drum beat and the classes marched away.

The treatment of the boy seemed terribly cruel to me, especially since the head told him to stop half way through because it was so bad, and recited the rest himself. When I asked Zainab about it she said this was the normal way of correcting someone.

The first music lesson was in the library. The reception class sang songs they had sung for parents the previous week. The children obviously enjoyed singing. They were dressed as sun and stars and sang nursery rhymes which I recorded.

Mr Raza in his music room in a school in Pakistan

This lesson was staged especially for me and was not the normal timetable. I did not appreciate at the time that they were singing English nursery rhymes in English, rather than Pakistani ones. They were accompanied by harmonium. I had not been to a Muslim primary school in England at this stage of my research and did not realise how amazing this was. At Islamia, a Muslim run state primary school in England, they only sing religious songs in Arabic; if they are accompanied it is only by a drum.

The second lesson was a Year 7 music lesson for girls. This was mostly taught in Urdu because the music teacher does not speak much English. There were eleven girls, most with short hair, obviously quite fashion-conscious; one even had dyed hair. Most sang quite well but one looked quite cheeky and didn't appear to be trying. *I later discovered that this was Saiqa.* Only two wore headscarves. The uniform for girls is white shalwar kameez trimmed with blue, with a blue blazer or grey jumper. *At the start of the lesson Mr Raza moved some of the girls around. I found out from Saiqa that this was so that I was facing the girls who sang well. So it was less obvious that the others, who were sitting alongside me, were not putting in much effort. When I looked, several appeared to be miming.* Everything seems very basic compared with English schools, especially since it is fee-paying. The music lessons are held in a tiny section of a very small library.

The library has few books other than a large number of new Oxford English dictionaries. *About 50 I would say.* The music equipment comprises an old Yamaha PSR 2 keyboard and what is presumably a record player – 'Latest model' Export Quality – it looks like something from the 60s. The lesson consisted entirely of singing patriotic and folk songs. I gathered that this was all they ever did.

Saiqa later told me that she found these lessons very boring and I must say I'm not surprised! When I asked about the Oxford English dictionaries I was told these had been donated to the school because it was felt that every class should have several. I gathered that they had been there for quite a long time. I saw none in the classrooms but did not discover why they were still in the library.

I was interested in the girls' hair because most of the Pakistani girls in the school at which I had taught had long, straight hair. Many said they were not allowed to cut it. This was not the case in King Fahad Academy in London, which is an independent Muslim high school. At King Fahad many more girls had short hair but they were generally the more Westernised ones. This fitted in with research done by Sharif (1989, p19), who quoted an 18 year old girl as saying, 'I was laughed at for the way I was dressed when I went to Pakistan... The girls there are far more fashion conscious than we are and the make-up they wear!' Similarly, I was surprised that so many girls were not wearing headscarves, although they did put them on when they went out of school. This may be because the school is considered part of the family. Interestingly this was an argument used by the school had I taught in, which thought the wearing of headscarves in school was inappropriate. The school had discovered that most of the girls did not want to wear them inside the school buildings, but their families wanted them to. They were told by the education authority that by not allowing an item of religious significance they were contravening the European code on human rights. This code is not applied in France where there is a ban on all items of religious significance in schools.

I would like to have found out why some of the girls did not sing. Some of the girls in my own music classes who abstained did so for religious reasons, so this may have been true of the Beaconhouse girls. I asked Saiqa but she said she did not know the girls well enough to say.

At home they listen to English pop music – Back Street Boys seem to be the favourite. *Some said they were allowed to listen to pop and the rest nodded as if in agreement, but I must remember that the parents of these girls have chosen to send them to a school based on the English model so are probably more open-minded as well as being better educated themselves. I recorded several songs.* All songs are taught by rote; there are no books. I asked Mr Raza, through one of the girls, to show me how he went about teaching a new song. First they learn the words until they can recite them, and then the tune.

A Year 5 (age 9-10) class came next. There was a power cut – these happen frequently – so they used the harmonium instead of keyboard. I think it sounds much better! Only half the class did music, all but one of the girls. The girls said they could choose whether to read in the library section or do music and the boys did not like singing. *The official policy is that half do music one week and half the next, because there is not enough room for them all at once, but I wonder if the girls' version is closer to the truth and gives Mr Raza an easier life?* The first song they sang was from the Punjab and two girls and the boy also danced to it. Again, most of the girls had short hair and only one wore a headscarf.

I was interested that two girls were allowed to dance with the boy. It may well be because they are only aged 9 and it is generally from puberty that dancing together becomes unacceptable. However, in Islamic primary schools in England I have visited, the boys and girls do not dance together.

The senior mistress thinks music is very important. Several paying schools do music but none of the state schools. She says Arun is very backward compared to Islamabad or Lahore, where the pupils are very Westernised and sophisticated.

Music in these schools means singing only. What is interesting is that if you mention music to a Muslim in England they often assume you mean musical instruments, but in Pakistan the word 'music' means singing.

A Year 3 class in an independent school in Pakistan

Year 7 girls' geography lesson. One plait, rest short hair. Studying the solar system, which they seem to know well, but everything is taught by rote. The girls all stand to answer questions or read. A concession to a more liberal approach is that they are encouraged to talk about what they know, but it mostly comes out in phrases learnt from the book. Zainab took this lesson and was keen to talk about it afterwards. *It was very difficult really because she thinks her teaching is very up to date, having done the 'Bradford' course. She talked about this a lot and rated teachers on whether or not they had done the Bradford course. I didn't manage to find out exactly what it was. Her teaching was not much like most I have seen in England and was based on learning facts rather than encouraging the pupils to think.*

When talking to the branch of the family living in England I found that one of the main differences they noticed in the teaching in Pakistan was the learning by rote. Akhtar and his daughter Anjum both gave teaching by rote as one of the reasons why they thought children did better at school in Pakistan.

Interviewed Shaheen Sabir, a history teacher, and Ghulam Raza. Ghulam studied singing with the famous singer Ghulam Ali. Shaheen's husband's family come from a group of fire-worshippers who were nearer to Buddhists than Muslims. They have now embraced Islam. Shaheen lent me two history books about Pakistan so I could read about Sufis, but these had been written in English for English children, in the Oxford History of Pakistan series. They may have been suitable for English children to get a flavour of Pakistan but I thought it was sad that this was the interpretation that the Pakistanis were given of their own country. Interview went well I think. Shaheen talked about musical influences in Islam. She had an explanation about how music was introduced into Islam in the Asian sub-continent:

> What happened was that the Hindu ceremonies, which were very musical with lots of dance and music, were very attractive. Music being a basic need of human beings it was obviously very attractive for people of any religion. Any religion, any caste, any creed, music being so universal it was very, very attractive for everyone which is very natural. So with Islam, seeing Islam didn't have any musical rituals, what happened was that the Sufis picked up a genre called *qawali. Qawali* are actually the praises of the last Prophet and God. [The *qawali* were adapted from the Indian bhajan.] So this is how music was incorporated into Islam.

She went on to point out that in Islam good and bad can be very close together.

> In Islam good is *halal* and bad is *haram,* anything which takes you to hell is *haram*. Once you slaughter an animal that animal is *halal,* but if an animal is already dead and you eat that animal that is *haram*. So it's how you use a thing, how you are using music. So, even in nature everything has a rhythm, a music of its own, so how can the nature itself be wrong or bad? That is the source of life, how can that be wrong? So it's only how you educate yourself, how you educate your children about everything, even about music, you have to educate yourself about everything. Some people link music with the bad. The only thing is to educate yourself about music. How can one even live without music?

Having the right intention is something which cropped up often, always with people with a liberal outlook. There seems to be a divide between Muslims who want people to think, and make decisions for themselves, and those who believe this will lead to a weakening of Islam. Shaheen was allowed to learn classical dancing as a child but not to practise at home, because the neighbours objected to bells jingling in the house. This made her parents feel uncomfortable so she had to stop. I heard this point on many occasions when interviewing children at Castle Community College.

Tasleem and Zainab were uncomfortable when I took them to a kebab house, even though we were curtained off from the male diners. I later found out that although they had been to a top class European style restaurant for a wedding they had never eaten out locally. I found it very strange that people who consider themselves liberal, as Zainab and Tasleem do, should never have eaten out like this. Although Tasleem would probably have gone again I'm sure Zainab would not. We all ate our food very quickly and left as soon as possible. Did Shoaib let us take them out because he felt it would be impolite to refuse? Or perhaps because he seemed to want to encourage his mother and sister to go out more.

Thursday 21 Oct. Tasleem is very talkative, pretty and great fun. She is rarely quiet for long and is really excited about us being here. Her English is extremely good, particularly her vocabulary and sentence construction. She is learning vocabulary from an American book and aims to finish it before she goes to university. She is already up to 'v' and keeps asking if she is using words like 'vicarious' correctly. Tasleem listens to English pop music and particularly likes Boyzone; Shoaib prefers Bryan Adams. The tapes we brought with us as presents were not a good idea because we could have got them for half the price at Abu Dhabi airport, and cheap copies can be bought in Pakistan. They would have been much happier with stationery and Bic biros. We took the tapes because Sunita, from the English branch of the family, had suggested it. She obviously knew which groups Shoaib and Tasleem liked because we did take the right tapes, but she did not know how easy it was for them to obtain copies in Pakistan. Almost all the tapes they owned were pirate copies, as were most of the tapes we listened to in shops. We spent time in music shops but were reluctant to buy pirate copies because of the quality. We later discovered that you could listen to them before purchase on the shops' high quality music equipment.

Zainab works very hard and takes her job extremely seriously. I watched her teach a couple of lessons. Since she is the school co-ordinator for English she is expected to correct the corrections of the other English teachers – I can't imagine any teacher in England being prepared to put up with this. Zainab cannot earn enough from her teaching to keep her family. A graduate teacher takes home Rs (rupees) 4000 a month which is the equivalent of £50.00, and a teacher with a masters degree earns Rs 5000, £62.50. Obviously this has to be seen in the context of living costs in Pakistan, but Zainab has to have contributions from her brothers-in-law to make ends meet. Many teachers give private lessons at home and can make as much as their salary again. Compared with most people in Pakistan, Zainab's family live quite well. Their servant, shared with the grandparents downstairs, earns the equivalent of £10.00 a month. She lives in the back yard with her two children, aged three and one, and her husband, who also earns about £10.00 a month as a gardener. They have two rooms but these are only shacks and have no form of heating, even though Arun has snow for about three months of the year. They appear to have virtually no possessions.

Shoaib is very helpful, friendly and fun, but he appears over confident and always knows best. He has been very kind, taking us to places when he really needs to be studying for his end of year medical exams. It is probably wrong of me to judge Shoaib in this way because all I know about young Pakistani men comes from hearsay. It would be quite natural for a girl at school in Luton to resent the way her older brother is allowed to control her life. Shoaib does all the family shopping, except when Zainab or Tasleem need clothes or shoes. He seems to be expected to go out for shopping two or three times a day; they do not shop in supermarkets the way we do in England. Tasleem has no money of her own so needs to ask for anything she wants. She says she would be allowed to go shopping in the bazaar with her friends but they do not like it because it is full of disgusting men.

This morning I talked to the grandfather, Muhammad. It was quite interesting, mostly about before partition, but not particularly useful because he either couldn't hear me ask about music, or couldn't understand, or couldn't believe that it was a subject of any interest! *Jumila does not speak much English but likes to come up and listen to us talking. This is difficult because it makes the conversations quite stilted. The rest of the family seem happy to ignore her but I wanted to include her in the conversations so tried to get them to translate.* It is strange how people assume who you want to talk to. Jumila was obviously thought to be of no interest to me, although I would have liked to hear her views. Maybe I was putting the wrong interpretation on it and Jumila did not have views she wanted to contribute. It opened up for me many different issues of social interaction and subject positioning and has made me think more carefully about responses I have had from other people I have talked to during this research.

After supper we watched television; a 13 year old girl was playing a harmonium and singing and her 11 year old brother was playing the tabla. Shoaib said that in Pakistan music runs in families and other people do not take it up. Although people enjoy listening to it they would not let their children, especially daughters, perform in public. Musicians have no respect even when they are famous, professional people. This gave me an opening on the family's attitude to performing, and he began by talking about acting.

For about 40 years there have been excellent dramas on stage and made for TV. State-run TV has rules so there are no conflicts with society. Shoaib says he would find it acceptable for Tasleem to perform in a serious drama but not to make a profession out of it. For example, she would have been allowed to act on stage when she was still at school. Tasleem thinks Shoaib would probably not have let her act even in a serious drama. Now Tasleem has left school, there is no chance of putting this to the test and I suspect that if it did come up Tasleem would say she was too busy. Although she works hard at her studies she does no housework and seldom cooks. We are still in touch and recently I asked her if she was learning to drive. Her response to every question is that she doesn't have time. Shoaib wants Tasleem to study away from home so that she can learn to take care of herself. This is a remarkably liberal view in Pakistan – not shared by her grandfather. Shoaib may be aware of how difficult it would have been for his family when his father died if Zainab were not a teacher.

Friday 22nd October This morning Rachel, my 16 year old daughter, interviewed Tasleem. As they got on well, and were close in age, I thought Tasleem might be more forthcoming with Rachel than with me, although she talked quite freely with me too. *She began by describing the music she likes, which is Western and Pakistani. Her favourite Pakistani groups are Junoon and Wild Sounds. She says many new groups are coming onto the scene. Pakistani pop music has been around since the 1980s but had little impact until Wild Sounds released a patriotic song about Pakistan in 1989. There is currently only one girl band in Pakistan. Tasleem says that most Pakistani girls are not into music. Tasleem plays the keyboard and her greatest dream is to play acoustic guitar. She envies Rachel playing electric and acoustic guitar, and says she thinks about having an all girls band. But when asked if she would like to play music seriously she said:*

> No I wouldn't, definitely not. People over here don't pay you much respect if you are a singer. Even if you are from a noble sort of

family with a noble sort of background and you turn out to be a singer, instead of an engineer or a doctor, they would say you were just an ordinary singer and on the streets and so on and call you a bad name.

Tasleem had harmonium lessons from 5th to 10th grade which is why she plays on the keyboard with only one hand. She had to give up when she changed school because the secondary school did not teach harmonium. Interestingly, she had lessons with Mr Raza, at Beaconhouse School, the teacher about whom Zainab is so dismissive.

More than anything else Tasleem wants to be able to ride a bicycle. She was allowed to as a child but it is unheard of for an older girl or woman to cycle. I had never considered the question of bicycles before, but now realise that the Muslim girls in Luton do not ride bikes. Tasleem thinks her family is very liberal. Her mother has let her study with boys, which is exceptional, but she thinks she would not have been able to if her father were alive. Her grandfather is not happy about it. She says many girls do not go on to higher education because they are expected to get married. She says it is impossible to find the time to study if you are married, but that things are changing.

> You have to make parents understand that their time is finished; I mean when they were kids they had a different sort of a time, different sort of things going on, but nowadays it's different. Everything changes with the passage of time and the up coming of different generations.

Tasleem said she thinks that Pakistanis in England are mostly confused. She watched a programme about Pakistanis in England which called them 'British Born Confused'.

TR: I have an example of my own uncle and aunt who have been over there. But they did not speak English. They just went off; started from here and started a family over there. My aunt couldn't even speak much of Urdu actually, she could only speak the local thing which they speak in the villages, they brought up their kids but they do lack loads of things.

RB: What sort of things?

TR: Things like... the kids, my cousins, their real emphasis wasn't on their education. My cousin, she's a teacher now, but she could have studied other things, things like computers but she wasn't aware of them. They didn't have the sort of thing going round the family which makes you aware of things like I'm aware of them. I keep on having a sort of attitude about my education that I must *be* something. My cousin teaches but she didn't have the awareness that she might have taken another field. And also her brother, I don't know if he studied very much but he got married at the age of 19, a very early age, and now he's about to have his sixth child. He's away in Saudi Arabia at the moment and his wife is having problems because she's an illiterate person and she doesn't know how to handle the kids. The grandparents are more concerned about the kids than she is. That's the sort of problem they are facing. The kids are so different from us. I mean, if I was in England I would be a different personality because I would be a bit more open, in the sense that I wouldn't be a shy sort of a person. I wouldn't be that. I would speak to my relatives more openly, things like that. But as soon as they come over they are like a bit reserved, you know, I mean they start talking to us within about two or three days but they are more simple. They are so simple that you just can't talk. I mean from England you would probably say that Pakistanis are not very modern but it all depends on the parents. None of them is into like talking to you openly about their life over there. People over here observe that difference and they're like 'how come?' I mean they are comparing me and them and wondering how come I am open and confident and they are so timid? People are confused, how come kids from over here are more confident than the ones living abroad?

RB: Would you say that's not what you'd expect?

TR: We definitely don't expect that. But then there comes the part of the parents. My mother is an educated woman who works. But over there their father is all the time out of work, he cannot find time for the kids and the mother has problems with the kids, you know.

RB: So it's been really bad for the kids that they are over there.

TR: Yes, definitely. They're not even confused. It's like they don't care, they sort of let it go.

Now I have met the English branch of the Khan family, this interview with Tasleem appears even more interesting because the people she is describing seem quite different from the people I met. They are all articulate and thoughtful and care about education, but maybe in a different way. I talked to Sunita, Akhtar and Anjum about the differences between education in Pakistan and England and they were all agreed that opportunities are far better for education in England, but that children generally do not do as well because they take it for granted. If they still lived in the village in Pakistan they would not have had many opportunities for education and would undoubtedly have been worse off than in England. There is a village school which goes up to age 11 but the secondary school was too far away to attend. The teacher in the village was only educated to matriculation (GCSE) and spoke no English. If they had lived in Arun with the rest of the family they would have done much better, as long as they could afford to go to a fee-paying rather than a government school.

They all agreed that although the fee-paying schools lacked the facilities English state schools have, pupils are made to work much harder. The pupils in Pakistan are far more appreciative of what they have and are prepared to work. Anjum said she would not like the pressure in a Pakistani school and is glad she is here even if she has not done as well as she might have there. Teaching in Pakistan is almost entirely by rote.

Ahktar thinks that the teachers in England now are not as good or as committed as they were when he was at school here. He believes that the Pakistani children do better when they are in a good mix with English pupils, and that the school he went to in England has gone downhill because it has become nearly 90 per cent Muslims, mainly from the poorer areas of Pakistan and Bangladesh. He thinks the competition from English pupils is good for them.

Tasleem talks about everything in a confident way which I imagine her English cousins would find off-putting. It is true that Fatima and Shazeen speak no English, but both of them understand it quite well. Shazeen even went out to work for a time. Perhaps what Tasleem has picked up is that the community her cousins live in would have come from villages in Pakistan and not had her opportunities. The children are much quieter than Tasleem and speak with a Luton accent rather than a refined American one!

Tasleem feels that Pakistani girls in England have a hard time when it comes to marriage. They see English girls marrying whoever they like and may resent own their arranged marriages. And many of them are marrying boys from Pakistan they don't even know, just because the boy wants to move to England. An additional problem is that if the girl in England has been well educated and the boy from Pakistan has not, it may be difficult for them to adjust to life together. This is the case with Tariq and Sunita. Although Tariq qualified as a teacher in Pakistan, this qualification is not recognised in England and he can find only casual manual labour. So he feels frustrated and thinks he doesn't fit in with Sunita's friends.

Tariq and Sunita had an arranged marriage in that Sunita was introduced to him as someone suitable when she went back to Pakistan on holiday, but she was not pressed to marry him and they were happy with each other. *Zainab told me they were worried about Sunita because she was 28 and had not accepted any of the candidates the family considered suitable. They were pressing Sunita to accept someone because they were afraid she would end up like Leila, who had rejected several suitors and had difficulty having children when she eventually married.*

Visited Ibrahim Khan and his family for tea – very English, with fruit salad and cakes but also sort of burgers and something in yoghurt. They put pepper in their fruit salad! Ibrahim and Mehnaz lived in Watford for two years, Birmingham for two years and Manchester for three. Ibrahim is a banker and worked in London when they were living in Watford. He said he was ashamed of the Pakistani communities in Watford and Birmingham because they were so insular. They mostly came from the poorer rural areas of Pakistan and usually spoke no English, and made no attempt to learn it – except the children at school. Ibrahim said they were tied by what the local imam told them and that they would never integrate with English people. He felt particularly upset because he thought most English people saw these Pakistanis as typical and he and his family were bracketed in with them. In Manchester most of the Pakistani communities he knew were professionals and academics. As well as fitting in better themselves, English people in Manchester, he believed, had a better impression of people from Pakistan. The children also much preferred Manchester, where they had a freer life and were in schools with a more balanced population – although being in their early teens when they were there the boys would have had more freedom anyway. If they come back to England they want to go to somewhere cosmopolitan like Manchester again.

Eleven year old daughter Saiqa came back with us and I talked to her about differences between music and dance lessons in England and Pakistan. *She came back to Pakistan when she was 8 or 9. She enjoyed dance and music in England and would like similar lessons in Pakistan. She says her parents would not mind her doing music except for the noise, but they would object if she wanted to be a professional singer. The Khans may return to England. All three*

97

children would like to come back but the parents say they would only bring Saiqa because the boys (14 and 16) have not worked hard so would be even less likely to work with all the distractions in England. The boys would love to come back to England because they think it is more fun and offers greater opportunities. Class, upbringing and home town or village in Pakistan are always signi-ficant: poorer families from villages find it harder than affluent people from the towns to adjust to living in England. Akhtar wants to keep the family together, and the younger children seem not to mind where they settle.

Tasleem feels it is acceptable to perform music but not for too much time because life should be more serious. She believes that Pakistani girls desperately need women role models, but most women do not attain positions of importance so there are very few. Any woman who is famous is a poor role model, for example Benezir Bhutto or film stars, although she says some people do admire film stars. Asked who Tasleem and Saiqa admire, who they'd like to be like when they grow up, Tasleem named her mother. She admires the way she lives her life but would not want to be a teacher herself. She could not think of anyone famous but said she admired Jean Paget from Neville Shute's *A Town like Alice*. Saiqa wants to be confident and honest but could not name a role model. I believe this is mirrored in the girls I see in Luton. Although women play a more prominent role generally in the West, Muslims do not see them as role models. Many girls in Luton are allowed to go to university but rarely away from home. It is still the assumption that when they leave school or university they will marry and have children and never work at a career. Pakistani women who work in Luton tend to carry out lowly paid jobs they can do at home.

This evening I went on to the balcony and listened to some folk music from a neighbour's house. It was amplified and very loud. When it stopped you could hear music from other houses as well. I thought it was perhaps because it was a Friday evening and they were celebrating after mosque, but Tasleem said it was just chance. The amplified music was obviously from a big celebration. The wedding season has just started so perhaps it was a wedding. Weddings are the main event in the Muslim social calendar and they usually have music. Men and women are generally separated but some liberal families permit some mixing. Sometimes only singing is allowed; sometimes there are instruments too. Although the music I was listening to was obviously folk, there were electronic

Girls doing their matriculation exam in a secondary school in Pakistan

instruments. I could not see into the houses the music was coming from so I don't know whether men and women were mixing.

Saturday 23 October. Today I went with Tasleem to the girls' high school right in the middle of the bazaar in Arun. In the entrance lots of women and girls were waiting for their relatives who were taking their matriculation exams. These are the equivalent of GCSE and determine whether they can go on to college. The girls taking the exams were sitting on a balcony with no tables or chairs, writing on their knees. They were fairly used to this because many of the classes had no chairs either. The school seemed to me to be in a pitiful state: the classes which did have desks had three girls squashed on to a bench meant for two. Only one classroom had any pictures on the wall and many windows and doors were broken. A small overhead electric fire in each room provides the only heating, and Arun gets very cold in the winter. Their main school holiday is in the middle of the winter because it is too cold to go to school. The library doubles as a staff room but since the only books they have are on a trolley this is not a problem. If a teacher is away sick, or on maternity leave, there is no replacement and four of the classes had no teachers. The girls were sitting in silence working at something. Four teachers were sitting talking to each other in the staffroom.

Some classes had about 50 girls. The girls were expected to wear white *shalwar kameez* to school and, unlike in the paying schools, all had long hair and most wore headscarves. Tasleem's aunt, Sunita, teaches Urdu and Islamic studies at the school. Lessons are in Urdu. The girls are expected to provide their own textbooks and stationery but are accepted even if they have nothing. They do the standard curriculum subjects, some PE and sing the National Anthem and occasionally folk songs during assemblies, accompanied by a drum. All the teachers are nicely dressed and seem cheerful, although they are well aware of the lack of facilities. There are some primitive science labs. All the teachers are trained and teach the girls by rote. There is no compulsory schooling in Pakistan but everyone is entitled to schooling from 5-16.

Many girls, however, do not attend, either because they are too poor to have the white shalwar kameez or because they are needed to work, or because their parents do not think education is important for girls. There are too few schools or teachers to provide education for everyone even at primary stage. If schooling were made compulsory the government could not afford even the basic education they provide now. This situation I found appalling. We see images of poverty on the television but nothing prepares you for being there. The problem of appreciating what is real and what is not unless you have first hand experience was really brought home here. *Shoaib told me the figures for government spending on education: about 3 per cent of the gross national product. A similarly small percentage is spent on health which, as a doctor, is of great concern to him. In comparison something like 70 per cent is spent on maintaining the army. I asked Shoaib how he felt about this and although he was appalled, he still believed the war against India over Kashmir was worth fighting. He said India would try to take back the whole of Pakistan if they didn't spend so much on defence.* I can't help asking myself why I think that music matters in a country so poor in so many other ways.

Bentun district in the North West Frontier Province has three girls' high schools but many more boys' high schools, 500 boys' primary schools and 200 for girls. Most are small village schools consisting of two classrooms and a playground. Usually only about 30-40 attend each school although in each area there are about 200 who are entitled to go (figures are for girls schools). They do some sport and sing the National Anthem and folk songs. Teachers who know nursery rhymes teach them, and the girls go home and teach their families, who love to sing them. At home they sing *lory*, lullabies, to their children. All the subjects are taught by rote: maths, Urdu, English, religious education and science.

Many families will not let their daughters attend because they prefer them to maintain *purdah*. There are no roads so pupils and teachers walk to school. Few of the teachers are even educated to matriculation level (GCSE), but now training is becoming compulsory. But once trained, they want to to teach in the towns, where the pay is far higher. Leila says that change is coming in attitudes to education – '*ilm*', Arabic for knowledge – but it is very slow. Adult education is available in the cities but it is mostly the young rather than the older people who want to study. In village society music (singing) is generally allowed as long as it is not linked to drink, drugs or loose women. Performing music is acceptable in theory but not in practice – everyone would prefer someone else's family to perform it. A few men and some women sing for special occasions, but separately.

At age 11 Tasleem went to the army school, the most prestigious in Arun and fee-paying. The girls' school is separate from the boys' school. The following is a quote from their 1998 school magazine.

> Music Club. Music is the cathartic expression of human souls. It's the medium by which poetry finds its way to the hearts of millions, expressing the nostalgia of the days long past, agony of loss and the ethereal qualities of love.

I love this quote! It sums up the essence of the subcontinent as I saw it in my short time there. But could you imagine this in an English school magazine? In my interviews and conversations in Pakistan the supposed lack of creativity amongst Muslims often arose, whereas creative thinking seems unimportant in the Muslim communities I researched in England. The magazine continues:

> Besides other clubs, we have in our College a Music Club. We have regular music lessons every Saturday during which students are taught the basics of music language, playing instruments and singing. Our aim is to help students learn more about music and also to channelise their talents. They are given impetus to come forward and participate in the Annual Day function.

All students have to join a club for one lesson on Saturday mornings. There are eight clubs: fine arts, hiking, Urdu literacy, drama, music, English debating, science society (physics) and English literature. Tasleem went to the English literature club. All girls in Years 5 to 12 attended a club, if reluctantly. There is a kindergarten up to Grade 5 which is mixed and the rest of the school is segregated. Music is not taught at all except on Saturday mornings. There is a choir and orchestra who play for Annual Day – although I did not see any instruments!

Went to see Ali and Samrina and their sons Abdul and Imran. Ali has spent some time in England and was in prison in Agra for two years after the 1971 war with Bangladesh. He thinks music should be divorced from social issues. He said we should do music which cannot be linked with social issues, though I'm not sure what he means. Samrina teaches Pakistani studies at a school for 14-18 year olds. This includes a course on culture, but music and dance are hardly mentioned except maybe occasionally folk music; it is certainly not seen as an important part of culture. If you want to learn classical music you really need to come from a musical family. They said there were colleges for classical music, mainly singing, but not in Arun, and it takes a lifetime to learn. They could not tell me where the colleges were, although they suggested Lahore, Islamabad or Karachi. *While staying in Lahore we tried to find out about music colleges but without success. I am sure there must be some but no one knew where. A guide said he would take us to see a famous musician who taught at home, but couldn't arrange it.* Since my return I have corresponded a few times with Hayat Ahmad Khan, the president of the All Pakistan Music Conference but although he has sent me interesting newspaper articles and information, he never actually answers any of my questions!

On TV this evening there is a pop concert. Those on stage are all men and so is the audience. The same does not happen for girls. There *are* mixed concerts and mixed audiences and if they are well organised Shoaib would let Tasleem go, as long as she was with a male relative. The same goes for visiting the cinema, Tasleem could go with a male relative but she says she would not dream of doing so because you have bad people in cinemas. She goes with her girl friends to dramas, parades and such like on the army base.

Groups of girls can go shopping unaccompanied but Tasleem does not like this because the men stare. Shoaib wants her to go because he says she needs to be more independent. Zainab does not like to be in public alone and always wears a *chador* when she goes out. *Tasleem has grown up with the idea that all men you come in contact with outside the family are bad. She would not even socialise with Shoaib's friends. However, men at university will be given some tolerance. Shoaib says that the girls who are training to be doctors get on well with the male students but they do not do anything social together.*

Leaving was very sad. Five years later we are still regularly in touch with Tasleem and occasionally with Shoaib. Both are now engaged and Shoaib has qualified as a doctor and has been in England looking for work but without success. When Tasleem went to university she stayed with family in Islamabad at first but eventually Zainab and Shoaib moved there as well. Zainab is still teaching in a primary school.

6

Castle Community College

This chapter presents a case study of Castle Community College, a large, mixed 11-16 inner city comprehensive in England with 950 on roll, of which nearly 90 per cent are Muslims, principally from Gujurat. The modern building is on an attractive site and exudes an atmosphere of calm and stability. During the Autumn of 1999 I spent time as a participant observer in the music department. Later I interviewed two local imams, an academic, and a governor of the school to build up a picture of the community based around the school.

The headteacher Jane Smith responded warmly to my request to look at music in her school and was supportive of what I was trying to achieve. But music needs to be treated delicately. It has to be included in Key Stage 3, age 11-14, because it is compulsory in the National Curriculum, but the school does not try to run it as an option for GCSE (Key Stage 4, age 14-16). Mrs Smith believes if it were offered as a GCSE subject parents would ask questions about its inclusion as a subject in the lower school, and might object to their children studying it. She pointed out that in many cases it is not the parents who object but the 'uneducated imams'. Nonetheless the school prospectus says that they hope to offer music at Key Stage 4 in the future.

After a long conversation with Mrs Smith I realised there were several difficulties in the way I had planned to carry out the participant observation. In order to minimise criticism of music on the curriculum, she adopts the attitude that 'what people don't see or hear about they won't know about'. Giving every pupil the opportunity to experience music is her aim but if she emphasises it too much she may lose even the limited amount on offer at present. Mrs Smith does not show visitors the music room even though it is well equipped and the pupils work hard. Governors are not allowed into school without permission and what they see is strictly controlled; she says they have several militant governors from the mosque who want music banned. She cited an example of the difficulties she experienced with governors: one wanted her to prevent the black boys from speaking to Muslim girls.

Music lessons seemed to consist entirely of keyboard work and there was no singing. This is strange because most Muslims who are not keen on instruments will allow some singing. Scarcely any pupils learn instruments at home and none do so in school. This may partly be because they have no peripatetic teachers. There was a black pupil who wanted to carry on playing the violin, which she'd begun at junior school, but to get a teacher for one girl was far too expensive. Mrs Smith was happy for me to go in but she stressed the need for me to get the approach right. She didn't want me giving pupils the idea that there might be something wrong with music when they hadn't realised it before, and telling their parents about my questions. By the end of the first hour I spent with Mrs Smith, she seemed more wary of me than she had been on the phone. I could understand why.

Music was taught by Charles Powell, who was having a frustrating time with his classes and was delighted that I was going to 'relieve the boredom' one day a week by sharing them with him. A second teacher, Don White, not a music specialist, also taught a few lessons of Year 7 music.

Music in Year 7

In Year 7 music is linked with technology and art and is on a merry-go-round, a system whereby the pupils have more intensive lessons but only for part of the year. For the first ten weeks, two classes have music twice a week at the same time. During the week they have two double and one single lesson, of which only the single falls on a Wednesday, the day I was at Castle. During this time they are spilt between Charles and Don and seem to have alternate lessons on the keyboards in the main music room and learning about notation in the second music room. I tried to keep with the same group so I could get to know them but this meant I was seeing them doing different work each time, which gave me little sense of continuity or progression.

As part of my research I planned to interview a group of pupils from each of Years 7, 8 and 9 about their experiences of music and their feelings about their music lessons now and in their primary schools. Year 7 music was on a Wednesday afternoon so I hoped to interview a group of volunteers at lunchtime after their music module ended. This plan did not work out because the date fell in the first week of Ramadan. I therefore interviewed them the lunchtime before they finished the module. Six of the eight girls in the group had enjoyed the module because they got to use the keyboards. No other reasons were offered. The two girls who had not enjoyed it said that music at their junior school had been better – mainly because they had played in the steel band, as had two of the others. With the steel pans they also had the chance to perform out of school and they had particularly liked this. At the junior school they had performed in a mixed steel pan group but they said that their fathers would not let them do so now they were at secondary school. It was the playing with boys that was a problem, rather than playing steel pans, which they all believed their fathers would allow them to continue in a single sex school. This confirmed my experience teaching at an all girls school in Luton with a large majority of Muslims. The girls there were allowed to play in school but many were not permitted to give public performances outside school. Castle has a set of steel pans, so it would be possible for the girls and boys to continue in separate groups, but they have no one to teach it.

It was obvious fairly soon that the girls who had come to talk to me were all keen on music, but only one played an instrument at home and that was the harmonium. Asked what they would play if they could choose anything, two said steel pans, two keyboard, two guitar, one piano and one violin. When asked whether their parents would let them play an instrument, all but one thought they would. Even so, music was seen as presenting a difficulty:

Sadia: It's [music] not good. My Dad said he wouldn't want music 'cos there's Muslims in the house and if people heard us it's not good. He doesn't like us having music but my sister's got cassettes.

Tasleem: My father doesn't like music because it's not using your time for something serious and you could be doing something for your religion.

DH: What about doing some sewing or watching television or playing with your friends, couldn't you be doing something for your religion instead of one of those?

Tasleem: If I did all my religion I could do those as well.

DH: So would music be alright if you did your religious duties first?

Tasleem: Yes.

When I asked if they listen to music at home, they said they like Indian music, meaning Hindi musicals, and pop music. They also like Indian disco music.

Sadia: My Dad doesn't like us listening to pop music.

DH: Are there any things the rest of you are not allowed to listen to?

Sofia: Anything with bad words. [Rest agree]

DH: What happens if you are watching something like *Top of the Pops* and a song comes on with bad words?

Group: Change the channel. Turn it off.

DH: Some people I've talked to say that when they are watching Hindi musicals they fast-forward the music and dancing.

?: Yeah – 'cos it's boring.

DH: Not because you shouldn't listen to the music?

Group: No.

Amina: Sometimes it's because of the clothes they wear.

DH: Why is that?

Amina: Just don't like them.

I had the impression that she thought they were bad in the sense of *haram*.

Four of the eight girls said they really enjoyed singing but found it embarrassing if they had to sing in front of other people. They thought they would like to do singing at Castle but preferably pop music. Sadia had lived in Egypt and a Portuguese speaking country in Africa. She wanted to be able to sing and dance Portuguese, Egyptian and Arabic songs. At the end of the tape she sang a Portuguese song. The girls mostly agreed that they didn't like Indian classical music or *qawali* but that some of their parents did. One girl said she liked a few qawali and they all seemed to have heard of Nusrat Fateh Ali Khan.

Music in Year 8

The school kept a list of all children classified according to their ethnic description, home language and religion. The Year 7 classes had not yet been classified because they were too new to the school. The Year 8 class I was working with consisted of 24 pupils and the breakdown was as follows:

- 10 India/Sri Lanka 4 Bangladesh 3 Pakistan 2 East African 3 UK (white) 1 Other Commonwealth 1 Not Known

- 12 Gujerati 4 Bengali 3 Urdu 4 English 1 Other

- 21 Muslim 3 Christian

Riffat, an extra pupil temporarily in this class and not on the college roll, was from the US and was staying with her grandmother for a few weeks. Riffat was a Muslim and provided an interesting contrast when she came to the group interview. Until this point she had worked quietly. She was not in the group of girls I had come to know best, but in the interview she spoke for much of the time.

The Year 8 interview was interesting in that the Muslim aspect was hardly mentioned. Although there were six girls present, Rabia and Riffat did nearly all the talking. The rest of the girls seemed to be in awe of Riffat and laughed whenever she said anything faintly amusing. On the tape only Rabia and Riffat's voices are identifiable but there are sections when several girls are talking at once.

Rabia had liked playing the tambourine and xylophone at junior school but didn't like the music teacher here and was mostly bored. They also did some singing but now she only sings at home with her sister, who has a tape which they sing to. They sing Indian music from films and English pop songs. When the group were asked if they liked music at Castle, there was a low mumble but no one would actually say that they didn't!

Riffat's experiences in America were very different. They did not have music, drama or dance on the timetable but pupils were expected to take part in classes after school. They had a chorus which performed in competitions. She described enthusiastically how once the chorus had made it into television. Here she misses her music and mostly just sings to her friends. There is no singing in lessons at Castle. The group were asked if they would like to play any instruments and Riffat again answered:

Riffat: I'd like to play the flute and my parents would let me. My grandfather loved music but I really only got to see him five times. There is a limit to dancing though.

DH: What do you mean by a limit?

Riffat: Well now I'm always dancing but when I grow older they won't want me to dance as much as I do now.

DH: What about at weddings and celebrations?

Riffat: There are circumstances – you can occasionally. When you get older it is embarrassing because people are staring at you.

The theme of embarrassment ran right through this interview, and might be attributable to their age. However, with Riffat it could also have been because music was unacceptable for Muslims. I would like to have asked about this directly but I had agreed that any mention of Islam must come from the pupils.

I asked them what they would like to do in music classes and it was again Riffat who answered. In America they had orchestras and cheerleaders and she thought they should try to make an orchestra here. The tape was not clear on the answers of the rest but there appeared to be no enthusiasm. They did respond to the idea of an Indian music and dance group at lunchtimes. They said that if they needed to have a teacher present it would be best to have an Asian woman, but that they would not object if it were Mr Powell. I think it unlikely that a male member of staff would be permitted to watch them dance. In my experience male teachers are not even allowed into the dance studio during dance lessons. None of the girls wanted to take music, dance or drama as a GCSE subject however much they had enjoyed it in Years 7-9.

Music in Year 9

There were four Year 9 classes on a Wednesday, of which I was involved with two. 9D consisted of 30 pupils made up as follows:

- 18 India/Sri Lanka 3 Pakistan 2 UK (white) 2 Bangladesh 1 East Africa 1 Malaysia

- 17 Gujerati 5 Punjabi 3 English 2 Bengali 1 Other commonwealth 2 Not Known

- 26 Muslim 2 Christian 2 Hindu

Charles began the term doing easier work with 9D because they had not done too well in year 8, but by week three he realised they could cope with the same work as the others. I got to know four girls in this class well. They often wanted me rather than Mr Powell to help them, and we enjoyed working together. They always looked to me to see how I was reacting to anything slightly different. Charles and I had developed a good relationship; he is very amusing, if sometimes rather sarcastic. With a new baby at home he is often tired, which means he can be short tempered. The class is aware that they have to watch their step. And he knows this class needs to be kept in check or they would quickly become undisciplined.

The girls were not particularly interested in music although they did get their work done. I hoped they would be among the group who came to talk to me but they did not seem keen when I approached them. In the end I did not ask the class for volunteers to speak to me because on the day I had intended to ask them they had behaved badly and it was an inappropriate time to ask. Charles told me about a boy in this class who wants to opt out of music for religious reasons but has not gone through the official channels to be allowed to drop it. He does not appear to be a troublemaker but during one lesson he was doing as little as possible and Charles kept him in to finish. I can understand that you cannot make exceptions for particular pupils, but it must be very difficult for the boy if he feels guilty about doing music.

There was one rather unpleasant incident with three boys in this class who were not working well. As I was trying to help one of them another was talking to them in Gujerati. I could tell from the tone of voice that he was being rude and from years of teaching pupils from this area I knew that at one point he called me a 'bitch'. I was not prepared to tolerate this and Charles took them out of the class. The boy who had been rude was reported to his parents and I thought this would now make dealing with him even more difficult, but he did not seem to hold it against me. I had the feeling that he was quite impressed that I knew what he had been saying – whereas I only understood the one phrase!

9F consisted of 27 pupils made up as follows:

- 18 India/Sri Lanka 2 UK (white) 2 East African 2 Bangladesh 1 Pakistan 1 West Indies 1 Not Classified
- 19 Gujerati 3 English 2 Bengali 1Punjabi 1 Other 1 Not Classified
- 21 Muslim 2 Christian 1 Hindu 1 Jewish 1 Not Known 1 Not Classified

This was a bright class who produced excellent work. They had worked well in Year 8 and Charles had an excellent relationship with them. Consequently the lessons were far more relaxed than with 9D. This class did much better than any other Year 9 class in the assessments at the end of the module. Perhaps the boys responded better to my help because they were more interested in their work, but I seemed to get on better with the boys than the girls. This became obvious when I asked for people to interview one lunchtime and three boys came along. All three were involved in music out of school and one of them began by telling me that they were a Muslim, a Hindu and a Christian. This was interesting because I thought they might be saying that their religions made a difference to their music and I hoped this might give me some interesting comparisons. But this was not the case and religion wasn't mentioned again. The point the boy was making was probably that they got on together even though they were of different faiths. All were allowed to do whatever music they liked. They had come to see me because they wanted more music in school and they thought I was going to be a new music teacher. One had learned the violin in primary school but couldn't continue because there was no teacher at Castle. Two played electric guitars and wanted to start a band. They thought that if there were another music teacher it might be possible to have some practical music arranged for them.

Music during Ramadan

For the last two weeks of the autumn term it was Ramadan. In 1998 Fortland City Council sent a letter to all schools telling them they should allow pupils to opt out of music during Ramadan. I had come across this with the occasional pupil in Luton but had not heard of an authority having a policy on it. The previous year 46 per cent of the pupils had brought letters from their parents requesting permission for their children to opt out of music lessons during Ramadan. With an inspection coming up, Charles was aware that he wouldn't be able to get his classes to the required standard for Key Stage 3. Although he did not go as far as to encourage his pupils to opt out, he did occasionally remind them that they had this option, because he felt that if they withdrew in sufficient numbers it would help explain the attitude to music in the school.

Abbas Khatun, Chair of Governors at Castle, was interesting on the question of Ramadan. He was partly responsible for the letter Fortland City Council had sent to its schools. He came up with an explanation about music in Ramadan which had come from scholars at the Iqbal Trust in London. They in turn based their ideas on information received from Dr Noyabe at University of Ibadan, called *Ramadan and Music.* Khatun quoted from the correspondence:

While music *per se* is not expressly forbidden for Muslims, during Ramadan music is focused on hearing recitations from the Holy Qur'an. Consequently other music is put aside during this period. Therefore all schools and educational establishments should be particularly alert to avoid offending Muslims. Moreover, one cannot guarantee that music played will not contravene Islamic law, especially during Ramadan where the emphasis is on spirituality and more to do with the sacred world than the secular.

Charles suggested that I speak to some of the pupils who opted out of music during Ramadan to ask them why they had withdrawn from classes. I didn't think it would be ethical to do this under the terms I had negotiated with Mrs Smith. She agreed that it wouldn't be right – but not only for the reasons I expected. She felt that most of the pupils really wanted to do music and opted out only because their parents want them to. She also thought many of them would not understand the reasons for opting out and it would put the children under pressure. I suspect that many of the parents would also not understand the reasons, because they had been told that music was bad without being told the reason why. The figures for pupils opting out of music during Ramadan are interesting.

1998			**1999**		
Year 7 Total	**90**		**Year 7 Total**	**97**	
Girls opting out	19	21%	Girls opting out	13	13%
Boys opting out	26	29%	Boys opting out	22	23%
Total		**50%**	**Total**		**36%**
Year 8 Total	**195**		**Year 8 Total**	**179**	
Girls opting out	35	18%	Girls opting out	43	24%
Boys opting out	46	24%	Boys opting out	52	29%
Total		**42%**	**Total**		**53%**
Year 9 Total	**191**		**Year 9 Total**	**208**	
Girls opting out	40	21%	Girls opting out	61	29%
Boys opting out	51	27%	Boys opting out	68	33%
Total		**48%**	**Total**		**62%**
KS3 TOTAL		**46%**	**KS3 TOTAL**		**54%**

More boys opted out of music in each year group than girls. This suggests that either the boys are better at persuading their parents to write a letter or that parents are more concerned about the boys' religious observance. The percentage of Year 7 opting out decreased considerably in 1999, which could be a sign of more tolerance but, against that, more pupils in Year 7 opted out when they were in Year 8 and the same happened as Year 8 moved to Year 9. Because music is not taught in Years 10 and 11, we can't tell whether this trend would have continued. This authority is the only one I know that has an official policy about letting Muslim pupils opt out of music during Ramadan. It is difficult to see the reasoning behind it. Hard line Muslims I have talked to are against music at all times, during Ramadan or not. Mrs Smith suggested that this may be a way for imams who oppose music to get children out of music for at least part of the year.

Non-teaching influences on music

I had asked Mrs Smith if she might put me in touch with some local imams, and maybe a governor, so I could find out more about religious attitudes in the community. At my first meeting with Mrs Smith she had said she would, but had not so far come up with any names. After eight weeks she decided that I was 'ready' to meet the imams and a governor, and find out 'what she was up against'!

Abbas Khatun has been a governor at Castle for some time. He is involved in other schools in Fortland and also does some teaching. His background is very different from that of the pupils at Castle. Although of Asian descent, he was brought up in America in an educated family. He allows his own children a great deal of freedom but has remained committed to Islam. Khatun has an excellent knowledge of aspects of music and Islam and is familiar with the work of al-Ghazali, the 11th century writer on music, and the modern writings of al-Faruqi. Much of the early part of the conversation centred upon theoretical issues. I asked him to tell me about his understanding of music in Islam:

AK: The word music is not mentioned in Islam. But there is some work done by al Ghazali, who explains the term as *sama* and lists music as a hierarchy starting with the *zikar* (calling to prayer). Actual instrumental music does not feature in music, only the human voice. That work is based on authentic sources. So really what we are saying is there is no notion of music as we know it because when you talk in the West about music you talk about musical instruments. So music out of the context of the *sama* is not clearly defined. With Muslims *sama* means listening to the human voice.

We talked on a more practical level about music in the National Curriculum and, specifically, music at Castle.

DH: So if we take it to a practical level thinking about what is required in the National Curriculum music statement...

AK: I would say that where music for Muslims has become problematic the cultural misunderstanding arises on the standing, nature, context, content and the general situation where we find music is located. So let's say if we listen to someone like Wagner or one of those classical composers, I mean I like *Sheherazade*, that's my own preference, it has certain memories for me of my boyhood, of space, of water, of a kind of experience of my childhood as I grew up, a reflective thing. So music has different meaning for different people but you have to realise that the people you are dealing with have not come from a culture of music. That's very important in your study, the people that you find will not understand what music is, they will adopt a kind of a pseudo, anti-Islamic position. Because Islam does not talk about Western musical instruments, they will believe that playing them is against their religion. As a type of creativity in itself music can be helpful in certain situations. So again, it's the application and the extent of the experience or knowledge of the individual who listens to it that will give it meaning.

DH: So in a classroom situation how can we offer this opportunity to all Muslim pupils?

AK: Well you have to look at the neighbourhood. In this neighbourhood you probably have a number of types, excluding Somalis and the rest who are a new intake. If you look at the main population here, it is Gujarati with a sprinkling of Pakistanis and a few Bangladeshis. The Gujarati group are not exposed to music or familiar with the form of music. From childhood as they grow up there is no definitive music in the house. There may be music from the films which people want to watch on the Asian channel because of the language and of finding out what is happening in the world and what not, and music is everywhere. You pick the phone up and have to hold and there is music, it's something which you cannot avoid. If you listen properly even walking down the road there is music and different types of sound. But at the end of the day, this kind of music, you know, piped, instrumental, voices, is a new phenomenon; it's not a phenomenon which people are accustomed

to. Then...you have a community here who are totally unfamiliar with music; music does not register with them, and if
you couple with that the fact that they are grappling with getting certification, trying to get jobs, then music doesn't compete.

DH: I understand that ...

AK: When I go to teach RE I go to different schools and I have to be
clear who the pupils are. There are white schools in the sticks
who have never seen a brown person and I have to make
adjustments for them and adjust myself for the environment I
find myself in. This is very unfamiliar territory. Within this
neighbourhood the highest point is to be a *hafis*, to be learned
in the *Qur'anic* exposition. That is what is valued; if you are a
PhD it doesn't have any currency. You know why I have currency? Not because I'm a governor but because of that little
time I spend in the mosque teaching those kids. In those two
hours I become a *mullah*, somebody who can articulate in
English, who is educated. But that is the icing on the cake: this
guy's OK because he can teach our children in the mosque.

DH: I perfectly accept that it's not a high priority but what I'm particularly interested in is trying to move forward in the school
situation. Music will be something that anyone being educated
in a state school will continue to be involved in. I would like to
feel that even though it is not a high priority, there could be
some way in which it was not seen as a negative influence. I
realise that the negative feelings come mainly from our pop
music because much of it is offensive.

AK: I'm a musician, I'm a professional bass player. Recently one of
my daughters came and wanted me to meet her friends...

Abbas then talked at length about his personal experiences and
when I tried to return to music at Castle he repeated that music had
no meaning for the pupils there, and resumed his thoughts about
what music meant to him. He said he does not feel less of a Muslim
for having musical skills and he does not try to hide the fact when
talking to anyone. He believes that music gives you a wide view because it is universal and links people together. He feels that music
gives you confidence and helps you mature and being good at it has
currency in Western culture.

I feel that as a musician himself, and Chair of the Governors, Abbas
is in an ideal position to encourage music amongst Muslims. He said
he would not play in school on account of his image. He didn't think

it appropriate and believed it would be misunderstood. The Muslims in the community would look down on him as a musician and think he was trying to influence their children in a bad way. From the point of view of the school, and from the view that encouraging music is good, this seems regrettable, because of the potential he has to influence Muslims who at present respect him. Part of the problem was undoubtedly that he is a bass guitar player and would be performing music of a pop/rock nature.

He said one reason why parents think music is a waste of time is that the children could not, as Muslims, be professional musicians. He said that even as a music teacher you would not take money for it if you were a good Muslim. Music is also incompatible with being a *hafis*, a reciter of the Qur'an, because it has a sound system of its own which doesn't mix with other types of music. Since in nearly all countries only boys are allowed to become *hafis*, I asked if this meant it would be easier for girls to do music. He replied:

> I think girls do things very differently in a way. They tend to be more active in the house. It would be very extraordinary, unless the girl was from a middle class family or whatever, not from this neighbourhood, it would be very difficult to imagine them doing anything very significant in music. I can't imagine it; I could be wrong. I don't say there is a problem with girls experimenting with music here. But I think outside of here they wouldn't.

The conversation ended rather negatively because he thought I would be unable to make music more meaningful for Muslims:

> We are in a time when Muslims feel that all the negatives of the world are coming together and society is being totally destroyed so people now are trying to save themselves. So music is more than just another activity, it has other connotations for them and that's the reality of the situation.

Imam Munir lives and teaches in the area of Fortland where most of the pupils at Castle live. He follows the *Deobandi* path, one of the most devout of the Sunni branch of Islam. My conversation with him began as follows:

DH: How do you view music as an imam, and does music play any part in your life?

IM: Personally, I don't listen to any music; Islam teaches that music is forbidden.

For Munir music is always linked with other matters which are *haram*, such as fornication, alcohol and drugs. He believes that within Islam it is necessary to do everything possible to prevent being in a position which requires you to listen to music. There are times, for example in a shopping precinct, when you have no choice but to be where there is music. However, he is a tolerant person and believes people are entitled to their own views and religious ideas whether they are Muslim or not. He is a governor of a local junior school and attends multifaith assemblies where music is played. Music for him refers only to secular songs and instrumental music. He believes religious singing is not only acceptable but to be encouraged, and would be happy to help with music in this form in any school that asked him. He has two sons who attend the local junior school. They take part in all lessons, including music, because he does not want them treated differently from the other children. However, when one asked to join the steel band he would not allow it because it does not fit in with the way he wants to bring up his children. When they reach secondary age he intends to educate them in a single sex Muslim school which does not have music classes.

Imam Beg, the second imam I interviewed, also has influence over the religious teaching of the pupils in this area. He seemed less sure about his ideas of music and was to some extent swayed by the older imams in the area. He was born and educated in this country and has a better understanding of some Western ideas. Although he believes that musical instruments are bad, and that the pop/rock scene is damaging the morals of young people, whether Muslim or not, he does believe that the next generation of Muslims will be more accepting of many Western concepts. His teaching is guided by the older imams in the area at the moment but he believed things will change when they cease to be active. This was interesting, and it was a view I had often heard. However, it may not necessarily be so, as he and Imam Munir are of the same generation.

Interview with Charles Powell

Six months after finishing the participant observation at Castle, Charles Powell resigned as head of music. He agreed to let me interview him about his experiences teaching music to Muslims at Castle. I began by asking him about his previous teaching experiences and whether he had anticipated there being difficulties. Although he had not taught Muslims before he had expected that, having served on a working party dealing with multicultural music aids, he would have been able to anticipate problems, but religious matters had not been dealt with. He believes all prospective music teachers should be given some idea about the situation for some Muslims in case they have Muslims in their classes.

I asked him about his first reactions:

DH: Can you remember your reactions when you were first faced with a predominantly Muslim class with a limited response to music?

CP: To start with I didn't realise that their religion was going to cause a problem because I hadn't been given this information when I was at the interview. So I went in expecting to carry on from where I assumed the previous teacher had left off and I got there and thought, 'Right, just get the discipline sorted out and then we'll do the music after that'. It was a gradual drip feed really until I realised it was not them being difficult behaviourally but a social problem, mixed up with religious problems. They never really were quite clear themselves what the problem was.

DH: Do you remember anything specifically which you thought was a bit odd?

CP: I think when they started to say things like, 'We don't listen to music at home'. I would say, 'Well you must hear music around you, what do you like?' and they would say, 'We just don't listen to it', and that started the alarm bells going. Again, I wasn't sure whether they were just trying to pull a fast one. But it turned out they weren't.

It was only when it came to Ramadan that he realised the full extent of the problems facing him and decided he would have to change his expectations of what was achievable. The biggest problem was in group work, which they seemed very reluctant to do. He was also led to believe that they could not do singing and was surprised when I said that for most Muslims this was less of a problem.

Charles also thinks that much of the fuss the pupils made about music was hypocritical. He said they 'often played the religious card if they were bored, especially the boys'. He told one class that if they worked hard he would give them a treat at the end. His 'treat' was to play some music to them – very little music is ever played. A boy with particularly strong Islamic views said that this wasn't what he would call a treat. When asked what a treat would be he said a trip to McDonald's. When Charles asked how he coped with the non-halal meat, he had no answer.

I asked Charles how he had decided that music would work best, given that it was on the curriculum and he had to teach it.

CP: What I decided to do was to set up the keyboard lab so that they worked either individually or in pairs, and had headphones. I wasn't giving them all the experiences that they should have been getting under the national curriculum – huge chunks were missed out. I made it clear to the management of the school, just to cover my own back basically, but they appreciated what I was doing and just said to do as much as I could. When I told them there was a problem they were very supportive of me, they didn't just tell me to go and sort it out. So, very much key-board based and we did in fact cover quite a lot of music but very much skimming the surface of it rather than going into it in any depth. The performing, on keyboards, went quite well and at the inspection two years ago the inspector reckoned that their instrumental performing skills were only just below expec-tations, which was quite good. Composition-wise, nothing – they weren't creative.

DH: But I did see you doing creative work. I know it was very limited but I thought some of them had a spark there.

CP: There isn't imagination and that's upheld in their English work as well. When they are asked to do something creative they tend to write something fact based.

DH: So in what ways did you change your curriculum?

CP: I really did quick dips into things. When I found that there was a tune or a piece of work they particularly enjoyed then I tried to do some follow on activities. So the curriculum evolved week by week almost, because I really couldn't work out what would take their fancy. We ended up spending twelve weeks on a Haydn Minuet with a class in Year 8 because they loved it and they decided they wanted to play it with both hands. They did amazing things; when they wanted to do it and were really into it they could do extremely well.

Charles did manage to get some percussion work from a Year 7 group without any boys he had taught the previous year. They had asked to do percussion work as a change from keyboards. He con-sidered this was the only time they did any composing.

I wondered how he saw the future of music in the school:

DH: In the light of all these issues, what were your hopes for the future of music or performing arts? Could you see any way of going forward, either as a discrete subject of music or in combination with dance and drama?

CP: I knew there was no way music could develop in the school because that would have given it too high an image in the community.

DH: I know that GCSE music would be problematic, but what if Years 7-9 studied performing arts as a combined subject rather than as individual subjects?

CP: I'm not sure that would have worked. Performing arts needs creativity from kids and I don't think they've got it or could cope with it. Drama was taught as a discrete subject and then was moved into the English group curriculum. Dance works on a modular basis where they do one module each year during PE. It would have meant massive re-staffing implications and there wasn't the money for it and so the idea was always shelved. There was nothing put forward on paper, there was no point. With my experience of it after three years, I wouldn't have bothered trying. I think it would be easier to do it with the kids if they had the backing from their parents and the mosques. I think the parents need to be educated as to what happens in schools; I think the mosques have their own political agenda and they don't need educating; they're clever people and they know what they are doing.

Charles noticed a difference generally in the attitudes of the girls and the boys.

CP: The thing which became very obvious was the big divide between girls and boys. The girls did pay attention and work in classes, and the boys didn't. This isn't just in music but in other subjects and the girls would read copious amounts... I think it was because they [boys] had preconceptions about what they would be doing when they left school and it wasn't really important to get a good education. They could either go into the family business or they might well be doing something with the mosque.

DH: So education just didn't seem to be important?

CP: No.

DH: But for the girls it was?

CP: Well, it was strange. Education was important because they wanted to get on and do it, but it wasn't seen as important by the parents. It was weird because the girls behaved well, for the most part, and they always got better results than the boys. The girls were not allowed out in the evenings so maybe they decided they were just going to go for it and do as well as they could because there was nothing else to do. And if they didn't want to go and help Mum around the house they had a good excuse if they were doing school work.

DH: Did you ever feel that you'd have liked to divide up the boys and girls?

CP: No. The girls' groups would have been a treat but the boys' groups would have been absolute hell.

It was quickly apparent to the music inspector that the National Curriculum requirements for Key Stage 3 were not being adhered to. After watching Charles teach two Year 9 classes, the inspector said that if he were faced with teaching these classes he wouldn't know where to begin. Charles continued:

He thought I was doing a good job. The other thing he said to me was that you don't knock something when it is working. So he could see that the way I was doing things would be problematic because of the National Curriculum requirements, but as it was working for these kids he wouldn't knock it. That didn't come through in the report of course...The inspector reckoned that in performing on the keyboard their skills were only just below expectation, which was good in the circumstances. In the report they were said to be 'below expectation'.

What did come out in the report was that, because of cultural issues, not all the curriculum could be taught; religious issues were not mentioned. The inspectors were well aware of the situation at Castle and in a meeting with the headteacher about what was going in the final report, she persuaded them to tone down their remarks about music because she did not want it made too public in the community.

I asked whether, now that Charles could distance himself from Castle, there were things he thought could have been handled differently.

CP: I think if the groups had been smaller there would have been more of a chance. With Year 7 I saw them in groups of about 23-25, sometimes down to about 18; 25 was the biggest group. I saw them for a double and a single each week for a 10 week block. Then they went away and came back later in the year for another 10 week block. I could do a lot of work with them but when they went into Year 8 and 9 they went into their teaching groups for other subjects and that meant 30 in a group and I saw them for one lesson a week. I think in any school you are then going to be pretty limited in what they can do unless they are really switched on to what they were doing. If you have to inspire them to begin with to get them going you've lost a lot of the lesson already.

DH: And how did you feel about having a Chair of Governors who was a practising musician himself and who never let anyone know that?

CP: I only found this out when you came to visit the school so that was quite amazing actually because he obviously had kept it very quiet. It's a bit sad really to think that a musician had to hide his skills in his community. He was like two people, it was really sad for him.

DH: What role do you think the junior schools should be playing in trying to overcome this?

CP: I think there is a problem in our junior schools because they have so much they are trying to deliver. As a secondary music teacher it's a real pain because you're not starting at the beginning of Key Stage 3, you are starting at Key Stage 1 or 2. When you do a quick hands up, some kids will have done singing and percussion and will be ready to start Key Stage 3, which might be a group of six or seven kids from the same school, and everyone else in the group will have done nothing.

DH: Finally, could you think of anything generally that might help other teachers who are in the situation you found yourself in at Castle? Do you see any way forward?

CP: Yes. I think being away from it and knowing I'm not going back to it, I feel less depressed. I think if you are going to be a music teacher in a predominantly Muslim school you ought to have some education given to you before you get to the school. You ought to be inducted properly.

DH: If you'd known more about the religion, would that have helped you because you could have put forward Islamic views in favour of music?

CP: I don't think that would have gone down well at Castle. You would end up with the imams coming into school and becoming a really big problem. My feeling is that if you go to work in a school where the Muslims are really devout, where they have real objections and they live their religion, rather than doing things they are not meant to do on the sly, you could respect that. I could say, 'That's really what you believe and I will not push this that much'.

Dance at Castle

During my time at Castle I attended three dance classes with a year 7 group. When lining up for the first dance lesson, one girl told me she didn't want to do dance because it was bad. I asked in what way it was bad and she said she wasn't supposed to do it because of her religion. She didn't seem inclined to pursue this so I hoped I'd get to know her better in the classes. Some of the girls talked to a teacher who was supporting a partially sighted girl in the class. They said that dance was not allowed in their religion and they didn't like it for that reason. I thought it would be interesting to talk to some of the girls about dance. They were happy to talk, but then since they had volunteered, I suppose they would be. Six girls from the dance module came, plus two of their friends from another class.

Of the six who had done dance, all but one enjoyed it and this girl didn't because it was the 'wrong sort of dance'. She found it difficult to describe exactly what sort of dance she wanted to do but had found the dance in the classes 'boring'. All but one other girl said they would be uncomfortable dancing in front of men and would not go to a disco. Several said they were only happy dancing with the women in their families, but it was difficult to tell if this was because they would be embarrassed or for some other reason. I did try to pursue this but did not get far and could not bring in the question of religion. Several said that their fathers did not like them doing any sort of dancing. I tried to get them to expand on this but they either couldn't or were reluctant to. If they didn't mention religion there was nothing I could do to press them further.

The current situation

In March 2005 I returned to the school to find out if anything had changed over the past five years. Music has changed very little in the school; there are still no GCSE classes but Jane Smith is hopeful for the future. There are still a core of people who are against any music but she sees the number reducing and attitudes becoming more accepting of it. She is hopeful because the school has done very well in the past five years and is now attracting a wider range of pupils from middle class backgrounds, including more white pupils. A white Year 7 boy brings his guitar into the office every week before his lesson. As she points out, 'you cannot work in a vacuum but if the pupils come from more diverse communities then you can build on whatever they bring with them'. Unfortunately they need a good music teacher and at present they do not have one.

The school has been successful because it has introduced GCSE short courses in RE and ICT for all pupils and gained excellent results. It is also sending pupils to the local college to do courses which they cannot provide themselves. These too have been very successful. Extension classes after school are offered in various areas, and these have also lifted the academic tone of the school. As well as the improvement each year in league table exam results, the school is also doing extremely well in terms of added value. Mrs Smith has been appointed to a high position in the community and this has had the effect of publicising her school and all that she, and the school, stand for.

7

Initiatives to promote music for Muslims in schools

The first of these initiatives took place in an independent Islamic school that was hoping to achieve Voluntary Aided status. I have not named the school although it was quite open about its policy to include music in the curriculum. The second was carried out by the School Effectiveness Division of Birmingham Local Education Authority. As well as presenting material at workshops designed to encourage more effective teaching of music to Muslims it interviewed groups of Muslim pupils about their views on music.

The introduction of music into an independent Islamic primary school

My rationale for undertaking this was twofold: as a researcher in the field of music education I felt I owed something to the Muslim community, who have at all times been supportive and appreciative of my work. And I wanted to be able to continue my research by looking at Muslim teachers in terms of their past experience of music and also how they would respond to becoming music teachers themselves. From the point of view of the Fatima Jouvaid, headteacher, there was another reason for the research. In September 2002 Michéle Massaoudi and I had carried out INSET (in service training) at the school. As well as talking generally about the situation with music and Muslims, I provided a workshop on rhythm, which I hoped the teachers would be able to expand for their pupils. On meeting Mrs Jouvaid again in October 2004 it became evident

127

had not happened and she wanted to know why the ...rs had been unable, or unwilling, to implement any music ...ons. I was asked to find out if, as she suspected, it was lack of confidence that was preventing her staff from teaching music. It was agreed at this stage that an evaluation of why music had not progressed in the school should be part of my research.

From my first conversations it quickly became apparent that the school was still only offering unaccompanied singing of *nasheeds* (Islamic religious songs) to their pupils. The school already had a music policy, although music was only being taught to the nursery and reception classes. Since the school was hoping to become Voluntary Aided in April 2005 it was realised that the situation regarding music lessons was in need of attention. Before I began working in the school Jouvaid wrote to the parents of the three classes I was to be involved with (Years 3, 4 and 5) to explain what the content of the lessons would be. At this stage it was agreed to keep it simple and I limited my teaching to pitch and rhythm, to be taught through listening, singing and composing. The school had already made an effort to include some performing arts for the children and had established close links with the a local theatre.

On my first teaching day Mrs Jouvaid told me about the responses she'd had to the letter about music lessons. At a school meeting, one father objected. He said,

> ...surely he did not need to tell her that music was forbidden for Muslims and that was exactly the reason he taken his three children away from the state school they had previously attended. At that school they were able to opt out of music and he assumed that they would be able to do the same at this one.

Being in the fortunate position of the school having a waiting list, and firmly believing in music's place on the curriculum, Mrs Jouvaid replied: 'No, they cannot. If your children come to this school they will do all of the curriculum'. She went on to say that all parents had been sent a copy of the music policy, which had been agreed with scholars and the trustees of the school, and that if he objected he could make a case to the next trustees meeting. A science teacher pointed out that there was a module on sound in Key Stage 2 science, where they did experiments with rubber bands and talked about pitch. If they did not do this module their children would be seriously incapacitated in their SATs (School Attainment Tests). One of the trustees said it was very important that the parents trust the teachers not to do anything which is not in the best interests of the pupils and acceptable to Islam. Mrs Jouvaid invited any parent to come in to a music class if they wished. The letter Mrs Jouvaid sent to the parents caused quite a stir; it was interesting that it had been discussed by several parents who did not even have children in the years concerned and who would not have received it. A parent of a Year 1 child said she was delighted that her children were going to have the opportunity to do music.

I decided that it would be much more beneficial to teach the teachers, so they would be able to take classes themselves, rather than simply teaching some lessons myself. I began by teaching a series of four lessons, with each year group in turn, with their form teacher observing. After this initial four weeks I went in every fort-night, the class teachers taking the intervening classes from detailed lesson plans I provided. From the summer term my role changed again and although I still produced the ideas for the teachers, they taught the classes with me as teaching assistant. Time was supposed to be put aside once a fortnight for us to all work together but, as is the nature of school life, this did not always happen.

At the same time as evaluating the reasons why music lessons were not being taught at this school, I hoped to research why some generalist teachers in primary schools were finding it difficult to engage with the music curriculum. The research by McCullough (2005) was key to my thinking. The teachers were supposed to be keeping diaries describing their feelings about music and the responses of their pupils but, again, time seemed to mitigate against these being as full as I would have liked. More useful were the individual interviews I had with the teachers, held twice near the beginning of the project and again at the end of the summer term.

This teacher – call her Rehana – had a mixed reaction to being invited to teach music: she welcomed the opportunity but was concerned about what was involved: both whether she could teach it and whether it would be right for her class and their parents. She was certain that singing and un-tuned percussion instruments were acceptable but less happy about listening to and playing other instruments. Four weeks into the project she was asked by Mrs Jouvaid to start a recorder club. Although initially unhappy about this she felt she could not refuse. Several other teachers told her that they would have refused to take the club because they were so unsure about its acceptability. Having talked to her husband she reconciled her religious views about playing the recorder, and five children from across the age range started recorder club. However, difficulties arose. On one occasion when the children were waiting for the club to begin they were playing their recorders in the playground. A mother heard them and removed her child to an area of the playground where he could not hear them, saying, 'Come away from those children. The flute is the whistle of Satan'. The school caretaker also caused difficulties for the children playing the recorder, telling them it was against Islam and was the work of the devil. Unsurprisingly the children were upset, as were their mothers on hearing about it. Mrs Jouvaid was angry with the caretaker and told him that different people had different views of music and he must keep his to himself.

By the end of the year Rehana was still worried about her ability to teach music but still convinced that music was important in the curriculum. She was concerned that she did not have the knowledge or understanding about music to teach it confidently but was prepared to have a go on her own. She was delighted at how much her class (Yr 5) had enjoyed it, saying:

> My class love it. They wait for me to write it on the board every Thursday and they really like it when we have an extra session.

Asked about what she thought they had learned she said:

> They have learned lots of social skills: how to share and work together, how to listen. Although these are important in other subjects they are absolutely essential in music. They've also learned some musical concepts, like rhythm and pitch, and they've learnt to enjoy music, which is just as important.

She was particularly surprised by the pupils who did well in music but had not shown similar ability in other lessons. There were some anomalies in the responses in relation to Islam. Some children initially covered their ears when Rehana played the recorder but later asked if they could try it themselves. In dealing with parents who are uncertain about music, she thinks it is important to explain to them about what happens in the lessons and to reassure them that there is nothing anti-Islamic. She thinks they should become more realistic and let their children have the opportunity to learn music.

The second teacher, Abdul, was older but had only just become a teacher. His family had not been particularly religious and as a child and teenager he had taken part in a good deal of music making. At university he had become more involved with Islam and was now a practising Muslim, but his views about music had not changed. He sees no difference between a poem and a piece of music without words; for him they are the same kind of creation and can complement each other. Although he is aware that some parents are unhappy about the music policy and about music being taught in the school, he is sufficiently sure of the benefits of music to want to be able to teach it. He believes that an intelligent person who can read the Qur'an is capable of interpreting it in an acceptable way, although he knows many Muslims would disagree with him. He said:

> I can sum things up in this way: if I look at a beautiful tree I thank God for it; if I see a beautiful river then again, I thank Allah for it; for me music just makes me think of God. It makes me think of the creator of sound and the order that actually exists in the universe, and it seems to me we are always seeking what it is that actually created us: the order in our bodies, the order in our minds, the order all around us.

Abdul is happy to be teaching music. He found that from singing to the children, particularly in front of other adults, he has gained confidence in all his teaching. He did not find teaching music easy, particularly the noise, and he had expected the children to have gained more from it. Looking at the situation from the outside, I think it was probably too much to expect him to teach music during his probationary year. I am sure he will find it more successful when he has more opportunity to interact with it.

The third teacher, Samira, was the most experienced. She had done a small amount of music teaching in the past, but was concerned that she should not 'teach the wrong thing'. Notation worried her, but she was happy about teaching music from other cultures and putting sound with stories. Like Rehana, she was surprised by how well some pupils had done in music. She said that teaching music seemed like a release from the constraints of the other subjects and enabled her to get to know her pupils in a different way.

Samira believes it would have been much more difficult to introduce music into the school a few years ago; musical instruments would have been completely unacceptable. She describes the present parent base as younger and more likely to have been educated in England. At least their education was less literal and less pendantic and unlikely to reinforced negative feelings about music. Some issues to do with music arose in her class: a group of boys put their hands over their ears if any of the girls played tapes, saying '*haram*'. These boys had not been difficult about music lessons but she didn't know whether this was because there was no pop music. Some parents she knows are still uncertain about music and she has encouraged them to come in to speak to her about it. Others, she said, have 'become resigned to it; they think it is safer to do music in a Muslim school than outside'.

Where lesson content was concerned I taught the basic concepts of rhythm and pitch in the first two terms. In the third term the children produced stories for radio, using sounds to enhance the words, motifs for characters and sound effects. I included some listening in every lesson, using musical examples from various religions and cultures from around the world. Not being a Muslim myself I felt unable to engage in relating music more specifically to Islamic religious ideas.

Music in the education of Muslim children

The rationale of the project in Birmingham differs from mine. Robert Bunting, the Adviser for Music in the School Effectiveness Division of Birmingham LEA, is the leader and he engaged Michéle Massaoudi and Sonia Gergis as its specialists. Michéle Massaoudi is a prominent Muslim educationalist and Ofsted Inspector. Sonia Gergis, a Christian, is an Egyptian musician and teacher who has considerable experience teaching music to Muslims. The emphasis in this project is to introduce Muslim music and culture into state schools with a high proportion of Muslims. These schools are all doing some form of music curriculum already but want to make it more relevant to their Muslim pupils.

The initiative began with a one day conference in February 2005. The objectives were to:

- gain clearer understanding of the range of attitudes to music in Muslim communities and among Muslim pupils

- be able to identify approaches to music teaching that are particularly sympathetic to Muslim cultures and values

- learn about some of the major Muslim musical and cultural traditions

The conference was followed up with feedback meetings where schools could benefit from each other's experiences, and three schools expressed interest in taking part in an action research project beginning in Autumn 2005. Amongst the most successful activities were: extending existing work on graphic notation to include material from Islamic art and architecture, introducing *nasheeds* into assemblies and using a story from the Islamic tradition as a basis for composing at a new intake day. The emphasis is not to introduce music into Muslim independent schools but rather to make music more acceptable to Muslims in state schools.

A second day conference for the teachers who already have the basic grounding presented in the first conference is planned around two options. The first group of workshops would present:

- more listening, plus further exploration of graphic notation
- more *nasheeds* to sing
- an introduction to Middle Eastern classical music
- exploring Muslim poetry and symbolism

The second group of workshops will consist of:

- a debate on different approaches to Thinking Skills
- consideration of the position of Muslim teachers
- feedback on discussions held with Muslim parents
- more detail about the different ethnic/cultural groupings within Birmingham's Muslim communities.

In preparation for the project, Bunting carried out interviews during Autumn 2004 with groups of Muslim pupils in three primary and three secondary schools in Birmingham. He gave as his rationale:

> I had become aware of the hostile, suspicious or ambivalent attitudes some Muslims hold towards music and wished to discover what impact this may be having on young people.

The schools were asked to select a cross-section of four to six Muslim pupils from across the year groups, with an equal mix of boys and girls (except for the girls' grammar school). The schools had the discretion to include up to two pupils with a specific interest in music if relevant. Bunting felt that since these were single interviews, and the interviewer a white man, it was probable that the children would be more at ease talking about their experiences of music in schools than in their homes, so he began by discussing these issues. This proved to be the case and most of them seemed very reticent about discussing music from their own culture or religion. Towards the end of the interviews with the older children some of their personal anxieties or difficulties began to emerge.

Everyone at the primary schools spoke enthusiastically about the music on offer in their school and all but one child listened to both Western and Asian pop music out of school. Two of the primary school groups appeared to have a good understanding of the more common types of music associated with Islam, for example the *adhan* and *nasheeds*. The third school were less forthcoming about religious music but this may have been due to a difference in terminology, *nasheeds* being known as *naats* in their particular community. The idea of music being unacceptable in some forms, for some Muslims, did not come out of any of these conversations.

The secondary schools were two mixed comprehensives and a girls' grammar school. Pupils at the comprehensives listened to Western music and Asian pop, and considered their music lessons enjoyable. Some at the first school were vaguely aware that some Muslims disapproved of music but felt it was 'OK if you don't take it too seriously'. The father of one boy with a particular interest in music disapproved of his musical activities.

In the girls' grammar school the situation was very different, possibly because of the two girls from Year 13 and one from Year 10 who were especially articulate. The whole hour was devoted to an intense debate about the moral status of music in Islam. It was dominated by the older girls, and three younger girls contributed their beliefs about the position of music. All six girls indicated that they did not listen to music because it is against their religion. They could cite *hadiths* and invoke scholarly rulings to support their positions. These are a summary of Bunting's findings in this school:

- music can gain control of your mind in an insidious way and lead to bad attitudes and behaviour

- music is part of the trivial distraction of teenage culture, linked with gossip and backbiting

- though acknowledging that not all music is associated with bad attitudes, they felt that 'music isn't necessary'

In the action research project designed for Autumn 2005 it is hoped that schools with only a minority of Muslims pupils can be included. It is considered important to focus more on secondary schools, where the relevance of music is more often challenged. At this preliminary stage in the planning, the following suggestions have been made: research tools might include questionnaires as well as group and individual interviews, but also 'research through teaching': sessions of listening to and discussing music of different types, to enable the researcher to access a wider range of responses when exploring attitudes. Interviewers should include people of Muslim faith and an ethnic/cultural background similar to the pupils', as this may be helpful in exploring the scale and nature of family tensions.

As a direct result of the research already undertaken, Bunting produced a handbook for teachers entitled *Muslim Music and Culture in the Curriculum* in 2006.

8
Practical suggestions

Music Exposed* is a publication written by Siraj (ibn) Yusuf Lambat (1998) with the specific aim of discouraging Muslims from taking part in music in school. But when I talked to him he seemed less hard line than his book lead me to expect. He was prepared to talk about the music he would consider acceptable, and said he'd written the book 'to put the other side of the question on music', knowing that he had given an extreme interpretation. Lambat asked me what the minimum amount of music would be to fulfil the National Curriculum requirements. I explained briefly the essential elements of performing, composing, listening and appraising and pointed out that how this was achieved was up to the individual teacher. This means that there is considerable scope for music to be tailored to the needs of the pupils. I asked him what the maximum he thought acceptable might be, but he did not offer any firm views. This chapter sets out suggestions to extend the music teaching in schools with Muslim pupils that I have gathered from the Muslims I have talked to, and from my observations of what is already happening .

■ Knowledge of Islam

Above all, it is essential that teachers themselves have a good understanding of the different meanings music may have to Muslims. Many of the interviewees suggested that all state teachers, not just music teachers, need to know more about Islam. As Kelani observed, 'If you don't know how your student thinks as a Muslim, how on earth are you going to know how he thinks as a musician?' You could work with a Muslim musician, although this has its own problems because in many Muslim countries musicians are not respected. Trevathan suggests bringing in a Muslim, preferably a teacher, to talk to parents about music and the ways in which it can be acceptable in schools. This could be helpful, as people are often afraid of what they do not understand.

Sr Ruqaiyyah suggested compiling a short publication containing the *ahadith* to do with music. It might include explanations by reputable Islamic scholars about why some *ahadith* are not sound. Pupils and parents could thus gain greater understanding of the whole question of music. Most interviewees thought Sr Ruqaiyyah's proposal a good idea but Ahmed offered a note of warning:

> It would be helpful but I don't think the time is right. At the moment all the world is going haywire about religion. I believe it would be right in two or three years time when things have settled down and people are not thinking the world is going to end and things like that. Religion will then be taken seriously again and a person should use it to benefit himself, to make better his own spiritual life inside. You can become a better person if you know the way. If you go to the gym then you can have a better body. Once a person learns the better way to a spiritual life they will have a better spirit.

■ Single sex lessons

Another issue is whether boys and girls can perform music together after puberty, or indeed whether they can perform at all. Although most Islamic primary schools do not offer music, many parents with children at state primary schools do not object to them taking part in class music lessons. I have taught many Muslim girls who have come to secondary school having played steel pans or even orchestral instruments in primary school. Some are allowed to continue as long as they no longer perform in public and if they play only in a single sex group. Other girls have had to give up.

Muslims are almost unanimously unhappy about the idea of boys and girls being taught together at secondary age. That most state schools are co-educational is generally unsatisfactory for them, but performing arts present a serious problem. There is a good case for teaching music and drama in single sex lessons in schools with a large number of Muslims, as dance is taught when it is part of PE. Extra curricular activities and school performances are greatly curtailed when boys and girls cannot perform together or to each other. Even in a girls' school, performing in assemblies can be a problem if male teachers are present, although admittedly this is an extreme view and often applies only to dance. But some Muslims treat the school as an extension of the family and will tolerate male teachers.

Massaoudi's main advice was that schools should be single sex. She believes Muslims would accept far more in terms of music within a single sex set up. She observed:

> The essential thing is that what the Muslims are trying to avoid is for children to become obsessed with music, as is the case with so many teenage children who do nothing but listen to pop music. It becomes like a drug in the end, like football for some boys. It mustn't become such an obsession that it would lead them to neglect their religion or their work or other more worthwhile ways of passing their time.

■ Combined subjects

Integrating music into other subjects has been successful in many cases. It is the idea of performing that is anathema to many Muslims, so it may be preferable to incorporate music into humanities, maths, languages and sciences where possible, teaching it factually. Musicians would say this denies the most essential part of music, but it is a way of introducing some aspects of the subject and will create chances for listening and discussing music. Styer believes that music would gain more relevance if used during the literacy hour and with performance poetry.

■ General content

Sr Ruqaiyyah considers the content of the music curriculum by dividing music into the five categories Muslims apply to all aspects of their lives: compulsory, recommended, allowed or tolerated, disapproved, forbidden. She does not consider any music to fall into the category of compulsory but maintains that 'anything which actually uplifts the soul, broadens the mind and brings you closer to God would be recommended'. All music which might be considered sexual or nationalistic would be forbidden. For example, although she thinks classical music would generally be accepted she pointed out that the apparently sexual manner in which Vanessa Mae plays the violin would 'strike a Muslim with horror'. National anthems are acceptable as long as they are in the form of a prayer, such as *God Save Our Gracious Queen*, but not songs glorifying the nation, like *Rule Britannia*. Any music which could lead to unacceptable actions or thoughts would be disapproved of, or forbidden, so this would rule out most pop songs. Everything else would fall in the accepted category, for example classical music or folk songs.

Thus it is essential for the music in schools to be carefully chosen to avoid offending pupils. I visited a girls' school in a UK midlands city attended by a high proportion of Muslims because it was the only single sex school in the city. Most of the Muslim pupils came from outside the school catchment area and had chosen to be there. The headteacher had made it school policy for all pupils to take part in all activities and those who objected were requested to choose a different school. Although this may be acceptable, something I saw in the music department was not. The class were singing a secular cantata about Ali Baba and the Forty Thieves, with comic references to his many wives, who were all completely covered. At the other extreme, however, many Muslims regard it as ridiculous not to play orchestral music about, say Romeo and Juliet. The complaint about this piece was made to me on grounds that it was about lovers outside of marriage, so suggesting premarital sex.

■ Aspects specifically related to Islamic religious practice

Musical examples should be chosen carefully particularly to avoid offending during Ramadan. I found that girls who were usually allowed to play and sing in an all girls school often asked to be excused during Ramadan. Sometimes this was for practical reasons: singing and playing wind instruments tends to make you thirsty and drinking during daylight hours is *haram*. Secondly, recreational activities are proscribed by some Muslims during Ramadan when thoughts should be solely about religious duties. Extra curricular activities clearly come into this category but should class lessons come under this edict?

Many non-Muslims are unaware that Jesus is a recognised prophet in Islam. Until the time of Muhammad, when the Qur'an was revealed, Muslims followed other religions. Christians, Jews and Muslims all follow branches of the Abrahamic faith, so all have the Old Testament in common. Hymns in praise of Jesus are acceptable, but do not expect Muslims to take part in music with specifically Christian content such as references to the Holy Trinity. Many Christmas carols are permissible, because Muslims believe in the Virgin Birth. It is important to include appropriate sacred music from the Western canon in class music lessons and, for balance, music from other religions.

■ Music from Muslim cultures

The school could even offer a module on Islamic music. Hewitt accepts that some songs being produced by Muslims born and brought up in the West are acceptable. Kelani would also begin with Islamic songs but she remarked that Arabs would be able to empathise with jazz and blues:

> It would really help if you have a school with a large number of Muslim students if you start teaching them Arabic music. Start with that or Islamic songs. When you talk about jazz and blues, talk about the human suffering. In terms of folkloric music, music of the peoples, the Arab mentality relates to these things.

Ask Muslims to bring in music from their own culture. For example, many people from the Indian sub continent will know the songs of Nusrat Fateh Ali Khan. When I interviewed Bangladeshi women in Tower Hamlets about their children doing music in school, they appeared unconcerned about music from a religious point of view but were afraid of their children losing their own culture if they only heard Western music in school. But it is not safe to assume that because music is acceptable to one Muslim family it will automatically be acceptable to others.

It is also a mistake, however, to believe that all Muslims want to continue to identify with music from their ethnic origins. And the heritage of some Muslims is located in the Western world. These two groups are often interested in music with a religious theme, such as *nasheeds*, but would like them to be in a Western style. Styer believes that many of the *nasheeds* used currently are not very good musically. He thinks that it will take some time for music to develop that is in Western style but with Islamic sentiments. He feels strongly that there is a need for good *nasheeds* for adults as well as children.

■ Ideas for composition

It is useful to have examples of Muslim poetry for Muslims to use for composition. *Muslim Poems for Children* by Mymona Hendricks contains poems about all aspects of Islamic life written in a metre and rhythm which makes them ideal for use when composing songs. Note that Muslims singing their own compositions might well be using quarter tones, and are not singing 'out of tune'. The fables written down by poets such as Rumi, which your pupils may know, can also be used as the basis of songs or for composing background music or sound effects.

■ Use of musical instruments

Singing is safer than playing musical instruments, for two reasons. First, for most Muslims, music is allowable when it is linked directly to praising Allah, and this means using words, unlike in the Western tradition where instrumental music is deemed equally to be able to express praise of God. Not only must there be words but they must be the main point of the music. This is why in most Arabic and much Eastern music, the only accompaniment is a single instrument playing the same line as the voice, usually without harmony. Secondly, musical instruments have traditionally been associated in the Muslim world with dancing girls, drink and debauchery. At my first parents' evening at a school with a high percentage of Muslims, I was astonished when a parent told me that in her culture only prostitutes played musical instruments. She was not intending to insult me, but I was shocked.

■ The use of ICT

Using computers or keyboards, and other IT related activities, often makes music more acceptable to Muslims. Many parents are keen for their children to be computer literate and some take the view that producing sound from an electronic source removes the performance from the child. Ibrahim Hewitt began his interview with me by saying 'I'm uneasy about Muslims doing music in state schools, full stop'. But he did admit that if Islamic schools were to be taken into the state system then some way had to be found to fulfil the National Curriculum requirements:

DH: So do the two Muslim state schools have to follow the National Curriculum requirements for music?

IH: Yes they do.

DH: How do they manage it?

IH: I really don't know how they are doing it. I know before the decision to give state funding was done we had a meeting at Islamia School with Meg Buckingham, the HMI looking after independent Muslim schools, and Janet Mills, a music specialist. We discussed how National Curriculum attainment targets could be met without using musical instruments and we said: 'Computers'. You can get all these computer programmes where you can make music on the computer. If you have that and you programme the computer to use the human voice and no instruments and you teach the children music by mathematics, notation, then they can compose and perform using computers. The dexterity skills they would get from playing an instrument they are getting by playing on a keyboard.

Massaoudi did not agree:

I know that some people have suggested the use of a synthesiser to reproduce the sounds but I think it's sophistry. It's also an unrealistic argument because at the end of the day you are still using sounds and melodies. If you are going to produce melodies you might just as well use the proper instruments.

Styer agreed with Massaoudi that using computers did not make music acceptable, though he would not use musical instruments either. He said:

On the question of using computers that is just splitting hairs. Since it is possible to avoid *haram* activities and fulfil the curriculum why use computers?

■ Invite parents into schools

Invite parents who object to music in the curriculum into school to see what you actually do in classes. Many have no idea – they have just been told that music is bad. Raza said that 90 per cent of the people who objected to music in schools had never been inside a school, let alone a music class. The myth that as music educators we will be playing rock music with offensive lyrics, or making children sing songs which are unacceptable to their faith, really must be laid to rest.

■ A word of caution

Mohammad Iqbal was wary of people who were trying to promote links between Muslims and non-Muslims too quickly:

What has really annoyed me over the past few years is that there are certain people – agencies – intent on forcing integration onto us. If only they would let it happen at its own pace things would be much easier. Sometimes they go about it with an almost religious zeal, almost on a campaign of salvation to bring people quickly to this culture.

■ And finally...

Shaheen Sabir, a teacher at an independent secondary school in Pakistan made an important point: central to the understanding of behaviour is *niyyat* (intention):

In Islam good is *halal* and bad is *haram*; anything which takes you to hell is *haram*. Once you slaughter an animal that animal is halal but if an animal is already dead and you eat that animal that is *haram*. So it's how you use a thing, how you are using music. You have to educate yourself about everything. Some people link music with the bad. The only thing is to educate yourself about music. How can one even live without music?

Resources for teachers

These are numerous, but I have listed only those I have found particularly useful.

CDs

A Dip in the Ocean Qasida Records (Moroccan Music)

Mercan Dede Sufi Dreams

Music from the Whirling Dervishes eg *Rough Guide to Sufi music*

Najma Ahktar *Atish*

Najma Ahktar *Pukar*

Nusrat Fateh Ali Khan 'Night Songs' A Sonic Presentation (only available in Pakistan but many of his CDs are available in England)

Reem Kelani *Sprinting Gazelle: Palestinian Songs from the Motherland and the Diaspora* Fuse Records

The Rough Guide to Music in Pakistan November 2003 Penguin Audiobooks

Youssou N'Dour *Egypt*

Yusuf Islam and Friends *I Have No Cannons That Roar* Jamal Records

Yusuf Islam and Friends *In Praise of the Last Prophet*

Books

Behrens-Abousseif D *Beauty in Arabic Culture* Markus Wiener, Princetown NJ

Hendricks, M (1991) *Muslim Poems for Children* pub The Islamic Foundation, Leicester

Rough Guides (1999) *The Rough Guide to World Music*

Further reading

al Faruqi L I (1982) 'The Shari'ah on Music and Musicians' in al Faruqi I R (ed) *Islamic Thought and Culture Institute of Islamic Thought* Washington DC

al Faruqi L I (1985) Music, Musicians and Muslim Law *Asian Music* Vol 17 Pt 1 pp 3-36

Harris D (2002) Limited Access Only: the problems of researching performing arts in a Muslim Pakistani community *Music Education Research* Vol 2 No 2 Sept

Muslim Educational Trust *Music. Muslims and the National Curriculum* MET London

Websites

www.mountainoflight.co.uk The website of Yusuf Islam's musical and educational organisation

www.cdwm.co.uk The website of Ian Whiteman (Abd al-Lateef Whiteman)

Glossary

Aqliyyaum – the community acquisition of knowledge

adhan or *Adzan* – the call to prayer

ahadith (pl) – the reported sayings of the Prophet

alal – action

balimah – a type of lute

bhajan – a Hindu religious song

bid'ah – innovation

chador – black cloak worn by women

da'wa – call, inviting people to Islam

Deobandi – a particularly devout form of Sunni Muslim

dh'ikr – remembrance of Allah

dogal – a specific mode used in Turkish music

Eid al-Adha – festival of sacrifice held on the last day of hajj (pilgrimage)

Eid al-Fitr – the breaking of the sacrifice at the end of Ramadan

fiqh – jurisprudence

ghazal – a song

hadith (s) – the reported sayings of the Prophet

hafis – a person trained to do the call to prayer

hajj – pilgrimage

halal – usually taken to mean 'acceptable' but more correctly 'obligatory'

handsah al sawt – sound arts

haqq – knowledge based on truth

haram – forbidden

hawa – knowledge based on desires

Iblis -Satan

ikhwan – associates

Imam-Hatip – schools in Turkey for prayer-leaders and preachers

imam – the leader of a Mosque

madrasa – place of study

makan – place

mubah – acceptable

muezzin – Muslim who performs the call to prayer

Muharram – the month when the Prophet died

Mujwaharis or Waharis – movements within Islam.

musiqa – non religious music

naats – Islamic songs

naqliyyah – humanly constructed knowledge

nasheeds – Islamic songs

niyyat – intention

oud – a type of lute

purdah – practice of keeping women secluded

qawali – Islamic religious songs

Qur'an – the Holy Word revealed to the Prophet by Allah

Ramadan – the month when the Qur'an was revealed to the Prophet

sa'ada – bliss in the after-life.

sama – listening to the human voice

sawti – entertainment

Shari'a law – the literal meaning of *Shari'a* is 'avenue' but it has come to mean the law based on the *Qur'an*

shehadin – martyrs

Sheihk – literally a learned older man but come to mean the preacher in the mosque

Shias /Shi'ites – the branch of Muslims who choose as their leader a descendent of the Prophet

Sunnah – the reported actions of the Prophet

Sunnis – the branch of Muslims who choose as their leader the person most qualified to be leader

ta'dib – knowledge dealing with character development.

ta'lim – revealed knowledge

taqlid – imitation

tarbiya – knowledge associated with individual development

tessitura – musical term meaning the range of a piece in terms of pitch

ulama – scholars of Islamic law

umma – community

wajd – trance

zaman – time, in terms of the time spent doing something

zann – knowledge based on speculation .

References

Ahmad I (2005) *An Open Letter to the Secretary of State for Education* London School of Islamics

al Baihaqi, quoted in Lambat Y L (1998) *Music Exposed* Time Publications, Leicester

al Bukhari (n.d.) *Sahih al Bukhari* Vol II translated Muhammah Muhsin Khan (1971) Islamic University, Medina

al Faruqi L I (1982) The Shar'ia on Music and Musicians in al Faruqi I R (ed) *Islamic Thought and Culture* Institute of Islamic Thought, Washington DC

al Faruqi L I (1985) Music, Musicians and Muslim Law *Asian Music* Vol17 Pt 1 pp3-36

al Qaradawi Y (1960) *The Lawful and the Prohibited in Islam* Translated by el Helbawy, Siddiqi and Shukry American Trust Publications, Indianapolis

al Qayrawani A Z (n.d.) Bakurah al Sa'd tr Russell A D (1906) *First Steps in Jurisprudence* Luzac and Co, London

al-Ghazzali (1058-1111) *Ihya' 'Ulum-id-Din* translated Maulana Fazul-ul-Karim (1978) Sind Sagar Academy, Lahore

Ahsan M (2003) 'An analytical review of Pakistan's educational policies and plans' *Research Papers in Education* 18 (3) Sept 2003 pp259-280

Allen (2004) Justifying Islamophobia: A Post 9/11 Consideration of the European Union and British Contexts *American Journal of Islamic Social Sciences* Vol 21 No 3

Association of Muslim Researchers (1996) ed Haulkdory *Much Ado About Music* Proceedings of Conference on Islam and Music London 1993

Association of Muslim Social Scientists *et al* (2004) *Muslims on Education: a position paper* published by AMSS UK

Badawi, Z (2005) reported by IslamOnline.net

Barenboim D and Said E W(2002) *Parallels and Paradoxes: Explorations in Music and Society* Pantheon, New York

BBC News UK (2005) website 1 July 2005 and 6 July 2005

Bowman W (2005) Research in Music Education Conference Exeter

Bunting M (2004) Muslims urged to embrace their role in the West *Guardian* 16 October

Bunting R (2005) unpub. Muslim Music and Culture in the Music Curriculum, School Effectiveness Division Birmingham LEA

Cook B J (1999) Islam and Egyptian education: student attitudes *International Journal for Educational Development* (review) in Cook B J (2000)

Cook B J (2000) Egypt's National Education Debate *Comparative Education* 36 (4) 2000 pp477-490

European Monitoring Centre on Racism and Xenophobia (2002) *Summary Report on Islamophobia in the EU after 11 September 2001*

Farmer H G (1973) *A History of Arabian Music to the XIIIth Century* Luzac, London

First World Conference on Muslim Education (1977) (proceedings) in AMSS (2004)

Haaretz (2005) www.haaretz.com 21 July 2005

Halstead M J (2004) An Islamic Concept of Education *Comparative Education* Vol 40, No 4 November 2004 pp517-529

Hendricks M (1991) *Muslim Poems for Children* Islamic Foundation, Leicester

Home Office Faith Communities Unit (2004) *Working Together: Co-operation between Government and Faith Communities* London Feb 2004

Hudson D (1995) Hamas rock's songs of glorious death top the Palestinian charts *Guardian* 15 August

Koran (*Qur'an*) pub Penguin Classics 1993

Lambat S (ibn) Y (1998) *Music Exposed* Time Publications, Leicester

Martin S A (2004) Multiculturalism in the Music Classroom, unpublished Masters Dissertation, University of Toronto

McCullough E (2005) Concept mapping: how to access and represent teachers' thoughts. Paper given at Research in Music Education Conference, Exeter

Muslim Public Affairs Council (2005) *The SUN Agrees Tariq Ramadan Is OK* 29 July

Pak Soon-Yong (2004) Cultural politics and the vocational religious education *Comparative Religion* Vol 40 No 3 Aug 2004 pp321-341

Ramadan T (2002) Proceedings from the conference on *Music Education for Muslims* London

Ramadan T (2004) European Social Forum, London October 2004.

Raza M S (1991) *Ilma in Britain: Past, Present and the Future* Volcano Press, Leicester

Richardson R (2004) *Islamophobia: issues, challenges and action* Trentham Books, Stoke on Trent and UBT

Saydam, (2000) *Flkogretin Muzik 8.* Turkey

Shirazi Ruzbahan Baqli (n d) 'On the Meaning of Spiritual Music' in Tahir 1998

Tahir R (1996) Musical experiences from an Islamic perspective: implications for music education in Malaysia unpublished Ph D Northwestern University USA

Talbani A (1996) Pedagogy, Power and Discourse: Transformation of Islamic Education *Comparative Education Review* Vol 40 Issue 1 pp66 -83

Tolkien J R R(1937) *The Hobbit* Unwin Books, London

UNESCO (2002) Institute for Statistics July 22

Walford (2001) Funding for religious schools in England and the Netherlands *Research Papers in Education* Vol 16 No 4 pp359-380

Walford (2003) Separate schools for religious minorities in England and the Netherlands *Research in Education* Vol 18 No 3 pp281-299

Williamson, N (2005) Music is part of God's universe *Guardian* 29 March 2005

Index